Becoming Iman

To Mo, Maya and Bear

Nacho: I'm a little concerned right now. About ... your salvation and stuff. How come you have not been baptised?

Esqueleto: Because I never got around to it, okay? I don't know why you always have to be judging me, because I only believe in science.

Becoming Iman

An Adventure through Rebellion,
Religion and Reason

Iman Rappetti

MACMILLAN

First published in 2018
by Pan Macmillan South Africa
Private Bag X19
Northlands
2116
Johannesburg
South Africa

www.panmacmillan.co.za

ISBN 978-1-77010-596-6
e-ISBN 978-1-77010-597-3

© Iman Rappetti 2018

All rights reserved. No part of this publication may be reproduced, stored in or introduced into a retrieval system, or transmitted, in any form, or by any means (electronic, mechanical, photocopying, recording or otherwise), without the prior written permission of the publisher. Any person who does any unauthorised act in relation to this publication may be liable to criminal prosecution and civil claims for damages.

Editing by Jane Bowman and Katlego Tapala
Proofreading by Pam Thornley
Design and typesetting by Triple M Design, Johannesburg
Cover design by publicide
Author photograph courtesy of POWER 98.7

Printed and bound by **novus print** solutions, a Novus Holdings company

To my children upon whose tablets indestructible memories are inscribed – thank you for never limiting me or guilting me into being anything other than the most honest version of myself. Thank you for needing my arms, my kisses, accepting my apologies, overlooking my immense shortcomings, and knowing exactly what I mean when I say think very carefully before having kids and getting married. You have enriched my life in ways that escape capture through words, even if I deployed whole forests and oceans of ink to carry out the task. I love you now and wherever the other place may be. Continue to sow kindness in this mad world of ours.

Contents

Introduction: Water and Earth   1

1 Enter Muhammad   3
2 My Mother's 'Pure Butter Rama'   10
3 The Wounding Years   19
4 Aunty, you Want Brass?   31
5 A Green Bakkie and a Biryani Pot   42
6 Craving Wholeness   48
7 Death Came at the Sink   57
8 The Sexual Revolution: The Back Story   70
9 The Blunt Force Trauma of Love   76

10 Ai ... those Brown Boys   83
11 The Yellow Submarine   93
12 The I Do's and I Don'ts   99
13 Of Prayer Mats, Head Coverings and Breaking up Family   109
14 Going, Going, Gone!   118
15 Chadors, Clerics and Change   124
16 The Night I Almost Killed the Party in Iran   136
17 Navigating the Slipstream   144
18 Clingwrap Sex   152
19 When Sex is More Cursory than a Handshake   163
20 The Unicorn in a Field of Lame Racehorses and Other Stories   173
21 The Sexual Revolution: The Rise of the Commanderess-in-Chief   182
22 And Now?   191
23 Which Face to Wear Again?   204
24 My Heart's Aperture is Wide Open   214

Acknowledgements   221

Introduction

Water and Earth

'I seek refuge from Satan the cursed. In the name of God the Beneficent, the Merciful.'

The words, chanted in Arabic, meet the water and mingle. The sacred ritual begins. Water and invocation, water and intention, water and hair and flesh, water over face, arms and feet. All the time the woman's heart is trained on the spirit, on the messenger and the God who sent him. Muhammad is the servant of God. God is merciful, God is gracious. She gets up and dries her sanctified body. She is ready to pray.

The rich smoke of sandalwood wafts through the room and curls up around her hijab. The long hem trails behind her and her burqa struggles to keep up as she races towards her prayer mat. If you look closely, she is smiling. She wants to beat the light and wills dawn to linger so that her supplication is in time.

Her feet glide over cold tiles and onto a plush, red musallah. The first one she ever owned. She stands; ready. The Ka'bah looks up at her. The ancient, black cube is richly embroidered on the crimson rug. She imagines she is there, touching its sacredness as she faces the direction of Mecca to begin her prayer. *'Allah hu Akbar.'*

This day begins as others will. She tries to forget the many before, in a time she regarded as the era of her personal ignorance.

1

Enter Muhammad

I stared at Ayatollah Ruhollah Khomeini and asked loudly, 'What should I do?! I'm dying!'

The serious, dark eyes of the Father of the Iranian Revolution stared back at me, almost disapprovingly, through his trademark bushy eyebrows but his mouth was firm and silent.

'A giant poster on a wall can't answer you, Iman,' my inner voice admonished.

I felt stupid, but desperate. I paced the tiny area at the front of our main street apartment in Iran's holy city of Qom. A lone cockroach also appeared not to care and lazily went about its business scavenging escaped grains of basmati rice under the tiny sink. I was in too much pain to go after him. The cheap, grey carpet squares bore the brunt of my anxiety. Up and down I paced in a shuffle of heavy, muffled steps. I fearfully gripped my sides as my swollen belly became the epicentre of lightning rods of fresh, intense jolts of the most extreme pain I had ever felt.

Minutes earlier the sky had prepared for a wardrobe change by shaking off its ebony and magenta nightgown and slipping into a sunrise sheath bursting with yellows and oranges.

The call to prayer had gently tapped on the window, carried by the amplified voice of the Muaddhin from the mosque nearby. 'Hurry to prayer, hurry to success,' it exhorted. I had done my ritual wash and the prayer mat was unfurled and ready at my feet. I made it through the first prostration but my swollen belly wouldn't let me go any further. Bulging with slurry amniotic fluid, it prevented me from connecting my head to the floor. Then the pain came. Then the fear.

My mother, Maureen, who'd flown out especially for the birth of my first child had already made her way back to South Africa because I had stupidly misunderstood the delivery date the gynaecologist had given me.

Anyway, she'd had enough of the city, and Iran in general, repeatedly asking me if my head was right. It didn't help that when she had arrived at Mehrabad International Airport she'd forgotten she wasn't in Dubai, but Tehran, and had neglected to put on her headscarf. Mistake. Big mistake, as she soon discovered. Immediately after exiting the plane, hostile guards shouted at her and marched her to the bathroom; she was bewildered and frightened and I think the old lady genuinely expected to be shot! She didn't speak Farsi, of course, and as she tearfully pulled on a scarf she was almost ready to go straight back home. 'You'd swear my hair was a bomb and could do terrible things! Hair! Hair! What are they afraid of?' she complained miserably. I chuckled privately as I pictured how it must have looked.

The plane ride between Dubai and Iran is hilarious. It's like the women on board have taken their hair for a picnic, an outing, which has now come to an end and must be packed away. Petulant coifs and curls must be tucked back and the scramble for headgear is a whirl of clips and slides till it's fixed in place. And ticks the box of what's acceptable.

I genuinely felt sorry for Mum as this was the first big trip she had ever taken. I soothed her and distracted her with that most delicious of Iranian sweets, 'gaz'.

So while she was undoubtedly munching on its sweet, nutty and gooey insides, here I was about to have my firstborn in a strange country, in a hospital thousands of kilometres from home and in a language I did not yet speak nor understand properly. I was about to become a mother without familiar faces and hands to help with my initiation. I wanted to cry like a child.

My copy of the infamous *What to Expect When You're Expecting* lay uselessly on the floor next to me. It was a lie. I looked at it in the same way a woman looks at a lover who has betrayed her. My water didn't break, nothing was going according to plan and who could remember how to measure the bladdy contractions!

I knew I would have to call someone. Ah, I remembered the mother of a friend. The only trouble was that I had only the most basic ability to communicate in Farsi. I was the butt of many jokes at the market, asking for watermelons when I wanted butter, or chillies when I meant meat and confusing the money.

I called her anyway but the poor woman was so confused so my husband and I piled into a taxi and headed for the hospital in the breath-suppressing heat of an Iranian summer. It was a Tuesday in July and we were about to become parents.

I had entertained no fantasies of a beautiful birth in plush surroundings so I was prepared for the bleakness and basic provision that was the Shahid Beheshti Hospital but I thought that hospitals in Muslim countries would at least be religious about privacy and modesty. It was not so. Well, certainly not in this hospital.

ENTER MUHAMMAD

Women were lined up on beds in rows facing each other with each person's baby-arrivals portal facing the next. If I sat up on my pillow, I could see right into the sister across from me and of course she had ringside seats to my most private parts. But this was not the time to care about whether things were tidy or how your experience compared with another woman. A stocky nurse with meaty, manly hands injected oxytocin into my IV to speed up contractions (read: hot, liquid, pain) while another pregnant woman feverishly walked past praying, calling for Imam Zaman, the last saviour of Islam, to please help her. It was a way of asking for strength and comfort. I tried in vain to tell the nurse, in the only coherent Persian sentence I knew, that I was close to death, and that I really meant it. But she disrupted the vapour of my dying breath with a wave of her hands and a knowing smile.

Minutes later she came back looking worried. The baby was going into distress. His umbilical cord was making an attempt on his life, having snaked its way around his tiny neck. There is a flurry of activity and a doctor from the university is summoned. Thankfully she speaks English and I am whipped into theatre. My last memory before slipping away was of the nurse's meaty, manly hands pressing down on my tummy with her entire body weight. I mumble, 'This can't be right, please …' and then disappear.

I wake up. Next to me is my boy. I can't believe it but I

am so tired I slip away again. Hours later I wake to the sight of his dad by my side, joyfully staring at the little life in front of him. He teases me, saying, 'I could hear your screams all the way down in the reception area one floor down!' Men are generally barred from the maternity wards in Qom, I'm told, so he doesn't stay long and leaves a few minutes later.

We name the life in the bassinet Muhammad Husayn. A name chosen in honour of a young man who volunteered for suicide operations during the Iran–Iraq War. He was just thirteen when he blew himself up in front of an Iraqi tank to stop it from reaching the Iranian border town of Khorramshahr at the beginning of the conflict. I had always planned to name my son Muhammad, in part to force my family to say it. To constantly drive home the message that I was Muslim and to get them to accept it.

At last, after months of ritualistic throwing up after eating platters of soft, fried chips drowned in yoghurt, black pepper and vinegar, in that mad craving of pregnancy, I could cradle the subject of my sacrifice. I touched his downy face and tried to imagine his future. His mouth searched for my finger. I looked around anxiously for guidance but aside from dispensing medication, the nurses expected there to be a relative or friend to help new mothers. I had no one. And Muhammad was loud and demanding. His cries scratched the walls and drew sympathetic looks on faces that also seemed to judge my inability to quieten him. I couldn't even communicate with the other mothers, let alone ask for help. My body seemed to rebel now that it had expelled its charge. My nipples refused to come out and sat there indifferently, almost as if they were watching the ward, seeming to focus more on blowing dry a fresh coat of nail polish than dispensing the royal jelly of colostrum and milk. The boy was hungry and searching and my bladder was tugging.

I put him down and took my first, tentative steps off the bed to make my first pee. Before my feet hit the ground, the pain did; I'd almost forgotten that I'd had a C-section. I took a deep breath and shuffled to the toilet. Pain. Pain. Pain. And then I remembered. This is Iran. I'm in a village. Long drop. I stood for a few minutes trying to work out how I was going to hold the drip, lift up my dress, tear down my knickers, squat, support myself and let go.

I gathered all the strength I could, crying as I descended, howling in pain as my stomach convulsed and the fresh stitches tugged meanly. Motherhood and Iran were going to be such fun …

2

My Mother's 'Pure, Butter Rama'

Maureen Jane Smith. Previously Rappetti. Previously Cumberledge.

We turn the corner into the street where my mother lives with a loud, proclamatory hoot that signals our arrival, as is the custom in this community. Hooting doesn't seem to be kosher in the quiet suburb where I live now with its have-some-consideration-for-the-neighbours unspoken protocol and tiptoed existence. Your noise levels expose your levels of class, or lack thereof. The quieter you are, the more civilised you are apparently.

Poor, fragile beings, they could do with a little spirit and a life. I often giggle to myself as I turn up the music at home for a spontaneous dance-off with the children. Yes, ja! Pump that Sister Bettina with its bass that bullies the windows into joining in as they shake and shudder to the rhythm.

I smile thinking about it as we pull up to Mum's house. Our arrival is an event that summons not only my family but sometimes the neighbours too. Coming from Jo'burg is a community experience. 'Kunjani Mtanami! Ulungile ingane yami?' the gogo from next door enquires, slowly straightening her back and putting down the greens she's picking from the garden. 'Yebo Gogo, ngiyaphila, ulungile Gogo?' I respond, meeting her eyes with a smile.

Then Mum emerges from the kitchen door and through the security gate. Then we watch her awkwardly shuffle towards the green metal gate in the backyard. She's managing a worryingly blue, sprained ankle while squinting hard, as if forcing her eyes to almost close will get them to see better. Her bony, white fingers sheathed in whispers of thin but strong skin, fiddle and fumble until hooray, she finds the right key on an unruly bunch and sticks its head into the lock, turning once to release the catch. Then she begins to bend and pull as I mock shout at my teens to, 'Go help Granny open the gate, man! Bladdy gormless children of today!'

As they giggle and scurry forward, I drink in deeply the scene before me. I wonder how many more years, how many more holidays there will be left for my mum to greet us in the way she has done for most of my adult life. I want to burn the image deeper than just on my retina. I want it to travel further, into the sacred recesses of my soul where joy, like fine wine, is kept in special vats. So that on a day in the future when she is no longer here, and I thirst for her company, I can stick in a ladle, take a sip of the vintage and remember …

Ha, but she's already outlived two of her children; she may outlive me too, I muse.

Her not church-on-Sunday hair is carelessly restrained by an old doek. Her high cheek bones, her cheeky, generous smile and eyes that twinkle with so much life carry the false guarantee of eternity in them. She's always half apologetic. 'Ey man, I must still jump in the bath,' she says as she presses down the folds of a well-worn apron coated in promising stains which hint at the fantastic food marriage that she's just officiated at in the kitchen. 'Ah,' I quietly moan to myself. A bride and groom of trotters' curry with beans, and their delectable retinue, a stack of 'pure butter Rama' rotis.

Pure butter Rama. That staple of working-class homes, Rama margarine. So good and dependable, so trusted, that in my mother's mind it is better than butter. I have tried arguing with her against using the margarine of our blue-collar days, and defending the superiority of actual butter but Mum insists, 'Vanessa, you can put all the butter you want, the rotis

MY MOTHER'S 'PURE, BUTTER RAMA'

just won't come out nice. Just use the pure butter Rama!'

You cannot argue with an expert. She is the original Kitchen Goddess and manages an impressive menagerie of spices and combinations with a regiment of yellowed wooden spoons (all stained by turmeric) and an alchemist's expertise. I believe her and I believe in the virtue of Rama because when I bite into those warm, soft, pillowy, light rounds of carefully rolled dough, which have been slapped onto a perfectly heated *thawa* (a special, heavy pan), flipped and then doused in dripping lashings of marg, I become a child again. I remember all the oil-stained clothing sacrificed in the hurried hunger for good, traditional, home-cooked food and treats.

Anyone who's grown up in Phoenix knows you have a special (old) shirt for plunging into the friendly, sunny orb of a local mango bursting with ripe, runny juice that coats fingers and forward rolls onto wrists and forearms. Or for eating their firm, green cousins with curry powder and salt in an optional bath of vinegar. Large portions of crab, fished out of the deliciously dark and mysterious pool of an Indian pot are notorious for spraying their spicy liquids as if the creature was determined to get revenge for its boiling baptism. And of course the gelatinous, silicone-like lip-sealing, thickly gravied T&B (trotters and beans). Kill me three times already, Nirvana beckons!

Lying back after the food orgy, with a glass of cooldrink

in hand (Stoney), before expertly launching a resurrection-triggering burp into a lounge full of protesting assorted relatives usually elicits shouts of 'Haibo! Yoh!' which is generally followed by snorts of laughter. Farting and burping were borderline condoned because the sounds and smells could become talking points. My mum would yell, 'Hey your'lls briefs will get torn!' as my brother Eugene and his always-ready accomplice cousin Earl, would let off a spectacularly jolting and surprising stream of cracks.

We did have rules though. A fart protocol so to speak. You got up, released at a safe distance, fanned your behind, or shook (both mandatory options) then walked back to the couch. Nothing worse than when the person heaves back down onto the couch and from below there is an uprising of methane and eau de colon.

But back to the gate. Sometimes it's my older sister, Jenny, who has the task of rolling it back and letting us in, almost always with a wry smile on her face, pushing back the stray hairs that have escaped from a tight ponytail to play across her forehead. My sister, unfortunately for the world, keeps her talents hidden from view. She can unleash a caustic but witty tongue, her special talent for singing (with an earnest singing face) and her ability to write brilliantly seem things covered in dust and long relegated to the discontinued series, *Forgotten Dreams: A Complete Encyclopaedia*. Like so many promising women I know. I wish her real self would come out to play more often but the hood has an insidious power to make chains out of familiarity and a paralysing fear out of the unknown.

This trip to Mum's house in the sleepy hollow of Pietermaritzburg is part of our family's annual holiday ritual. It's en route to our compulsory ocean worship service at North Beach. No visit to the coast feels whole unless there is a stop at the tiny house, which swells with abundance enough to pole vault over a skyscraper. It's always been like that.

Mum jokes, 'Ey Vanessa, I try to cook small but it always comes out big, you know? I'm so used of that.' Recently, following the death of my Uncle Reggie, Mum only has to cook for herself. It was Uncle Reggie that helped soothe her heartache after my father died and reminded her how to love again. Their wedding at our old church in Durban was a joyous affair decorated with confetti and congratulations, even though the last significant occasion we had attended in that same place was the dramatic send-off at my father's funeral. Full circles are strange things, aren't they? The way a story begins, arcs and ends can answer old questions and create a sense of completion. Mum had met Uncle Reggie before my father, falling in love with the bus driver and creating my sister and here, years later, could continue their story writing a fresh chapter in their very own book of romance.

But old habits die hard. Her hand still chooses a whole onion and what's the point of frying 'just one chop?' My mother can't do it. Generosity, muchness have been her habits. And by osmosis, I have them too.

By now the five-hour drive, monotonous 'I spy' and guessing games have made us all more than ready to close the endless distance between the car and the table. Mummy ushers us inside where it becomes a Cirque du Soleil of juggling crockery and disappearing food, till all that looks up at you from the traumatised plate are the whitest bones, licked dry and sticky fingers itching to dish up the next round.

Mum laughs at my reactions which are part ecstasy, part drama as spoonfuls of beans march dutifully across the threshold of my mouth waiting to be joined by cooked feet suspended just millimetres from my lips, 'Come to mamma you pretty, heavenly hooves, you can't run from me now!'

Her enjoyment is very audible. My mother's laugh is somewhere between gurgling drain, machine gunfire and worrying wheeze, when she's really having fun. Her body convulses concerningly (she's seventy now and seems smaller, more fragile) but she breaks out with gusto.

I remember once, during a particularly awkward screening of *101 Reykjavik* at the Gay and Lesbian Film Festival, that I should have known better than to take my mum to, who is somewhere in that delicate place between 'saved' sensibilities and tentative boundary pushing and liberal exploration, a particularly steamy scene where two women bare their passion for each other in a dance studio. The naked boobs and eager lips triggered my mother into uncontrollable laughter, more out of shock than mirth. It seemed as if the entire theatre, in miraculously perfect synchronicity, looked around to identify the disturbance. As eyes burnt into the top of my head (which by now is bowed and forensically examining whether the popcorn to salt ratio is perfect), I wanted a black hole to emerge and abduct me.

Now that I'm older, I'm less bothered by the things my mother does. Her loudness, spontaneous kindness (she'll give away the shirt on her back if asked) and ability to have a roaring conversation with a complete stranger show me that her confidence is high, that through all the hardships she's experienced, her spirit is not broken. She has taught me to care less what people think and more about what I think of myself.

I am reminded of a time when I was much younger when I would resist and protest her love for blood-red lipstick. I thought it was too much, too loud, too attention-seeking, especially for a person whose thin lips were more suggestion than fact. But she would insist it made her feel good and I eventually let it go. Now I can't picture her in anything but her signature siren-spinning colour. When I watch her get ready, puckering her lips, sliding on the magical red, it is her happy, self-congratulatory eyes in the mirror that confirm her sense of pride. My mother loves to dress up. Often, after Sunday morning service, she'll phone me and I can hear the smile in her voice. 'Ey, I looked so nice this morning the sisters couldn't get over it.' She recently called to say she needed a new outfit for a wedding. When I reminded her that her wardrobe, like the country, was heaving with possibilities, she laughed and said, 'Hau, but they all saw that, didn't I wear that to what's-its-name's funeral? I have to be fresh, you know, I'm old but I'm not cold.'

And there again, another lesson. This sister still has it going on, twice a widow and still her fire burns. Rumour has it there could be a romance again in her future but I'm not telling. What it means is that if my mum is rocking it there's hope for the likes of me …

3

The Wounding Years

Every time the wind took a mighty breath and launched itself against the metal garage door that stood between our bedroom and outside, it would convulse and determined dust particles would leopard crawl through the space just under its heavy lip. No amount of old towels or wads of rolled-up newspaper could stop them coming inside. And every day I would moan and click loudly as I stooped, my back burning, heavy bucket and straggly mop in hand, trying to banish the particles to non-existence. Again. Like I did yesterday. And every day before that. A ten-year-old fighting a losing battle against nature.

The garage cottage was our home for a few years. It was located at the bottom of a dusty driveway belonging to a big house at the end of the long and winding Fulham Road. The posh-sounding Indian suburb of Reservoir Hills (Reser-Voo-Waaah, darling) lived up to its name as sprawling (sometimes gaudy) mansions dotted the dense, green hills of KwaZulu-Natal and big, shiny cars lazily sunned themselves in front of fancy entrances. This is where the Indian community's educated or business-minded were able to settle in significant comfort.

For families like ours, families of meagre means, an outbuilding was the only affordable option in the area. My parents were struggling, following my father's heated and vulgar excommunication from his wealthy family's fresh produce empire as punishment for marrying a 'coloured' woman. After all, the Rapitis were from 'pure-blooded' stock all the way, from the old country in a suburb called Anakapalle (known for its jaggery, a hard, concentrated sugar cane used in the making of delicious sweetmeats) nestled in a port city called Visakhapatnam in the Indian state of Andhra Pradesh. People have sometimes asked me (when they are not confusing my surname for being Italian) whether I am Andhra but first let me say that the journey from Rapiti to Rappetti is as bland and as undramatic as a Home Affairs bungle which my parents just let go of. Perhaps in some subconscious way it served as a marker for the separation our family felt from the rest of the clan. So the question of whether I am Andra was always posed with a sense of 'oooh, aaah' pride and superiority, like it's a special pure 'breed' or class. The exceptionalism always went over my head. I didn't understand why it would be something special. I learnt later that all it really denotes is a geographical area in India. But I began to understand that what I thought was exceptionalism, had more to do with a sense of kin and brotherhood, about a place many of my grandparents' peers and parents were torn from. Whole families that found themselves heading to a life of hard labour, of sweating and slashing the rigid stalks of sugar cane in KwaZulu-Natal's plantations. The question also piqued my interest in pursuing the possibility that we might have some family somewhere far away that we have never met who could perhaps tell us more about our ancestors and the gaping hole created by the great forced labour exodus.

The insignificant detail of them having been brought over as infants on the SS Munroe XL with their parents who were part of that murky indentured labour programme was not mentioned. All that mattered was that they were from somewhere else. Isn't it funny how 'You know where we're originally from?' has an exotic ring to it, when in reality it could actually be as parochial as the place where you are currently living. But let's not let the facts stand in the way … and all that …

My father's expulsion from his family was as firm as jelly because of course my Amma (his mother) cried for him to visit. Gradually he began to go to her and so my mum and us kids saw more of the grand old lady. She was an impressive, commanding force. Her skin was that of the rich darkness of tamarind paste and across her face the engravings of mysterious tattoos teased at their hidden meanings. You had to look closely to see the faded green lines and curves. She spoke mostly in Telugu, expertly balancing words and restraining the crimson saliva churned up by the almost never-ending chewing of betel nut, lime and betel leaves. She would signal for us to come to her and we would squat down next to her, staring in wonder at her solid gold *thali*, which was more rope than necklace (very expensive, you know). My grandfather had died after a series of leg amputations failed to arrest the march of gangrene and so she wore the white sari of widowhood. Conspiratorially, she would reach inside the folds for a secret compartment that concealed a knotted, white handkerchief.

Our eyes would widen in expectation for the big, shiny one rand coin hidden in the fabric that would be dispensed from fingers heavy with gold. We would scurry off like pirates with their loot, already spending it in our heads on chips and 'mindrals' (cooldrinks) but not before Amma had something to say.

A lamentation in heavily accented English would usually follow; 'Venesha, why you don't brush your hair, why you don't tie a plait?' Of course my tight curls could never achieve any real, celebration-worthy length and would never pretend to be straight, so visions of that long, envy-inducing, Amma-appeasing plait, that would bounce off my buttocks to the strains of a hypnotic Bollywood number played in slow motion, were poorly placed. It took the shine off my coin. I would slink away and vow to drown my hair in Amla oil (the green one) and light a god lamp and pray for it to reach my ankles (as if!).

We would make the occasional visit to my father's family in the Big House On The Hill to swim in their pool (a rare luxury in those days) which would unfortunately put my mother in direct line of sight of my father's sisters and brothers (not all of them, mind you) who showed her no mercy. They were relentless in their racist and judgemental persecution. The evidence of how deep it hurt her, lies in the fact that to this day the memory of a conversation, altercation and ridicule seems as fresh and unhealed as the day it happened.

At one point growing up I remember thinking that all they thought she was good for was making a milk tart (hers is really a celestially, custardy thing of beauty).

But Maureen was somehow never good enough for them even though she tried really hard. I remember her being in hospital having a lump removed from her neck and I was being babysat by my aunties. It wasn't long after the door closed on my father's return to work that I had to endure their sneering commentary about how useless my mother was. I vividly recall sitting on the floor of their apartment in Puntans Hill and listening to their suggestions that she was a loose woman who had trapped my father. You can picture the scene, right? Just a bit of frivolous and light late-afternoon banter to distract a child who is worried her mother might die under the knife.

Back at the cottage on Fulham Road my brother and I made ourselves as comfortable as possible even if it meant sharing a bedroom with our parents with only a set of (hideous) red and black wardrobes between us. Like with many families who have to make small spaces work for them, the things you take for granted become important. My parents had to dial back any intimacy. I'm sure that when the urge hit them they parked their passion until after lights out and deployed it with the expertise of mime artists. It makes me laugh thinking about it now as an adult, who herself is prone to pretty loud gasping, of how much of a challenge it would have been for my parents.

It's funny how, like with most poor families, privacy is a very distant cousin of poverty. You don't get to have secrets when you're all lumped together like dumplings crammed into a stew pot. Because the one thing cheap wardrobes and flimsy curtains could not conceal was the hot fire of jealousy that seemed to boil inside my father and spill out of him like leaking, destructive lava.

In the early days of their marriage, before the advent of Jesus and his power to transform the wicked, my father used to 'see' affairs in those wardrobes, behind doors and under beds. An innocent smile from my mother to a stranger seemed, in his mind, to be confirmation of tangled sheets, sweaty pulsating bodies and pure betrayal. So the meeting of fist and face, boot and back were inevitable when they got home. That was the cycle; with ever more predictable regularity.

Despite putting up a rickety, united front to family and friends the fights between them and my mother's 'Colouredness' and my fathers 'Indianness' were their only weapons of destruction. Sometimes it didn't matter whether the fight originated over burnt curries or burnt feelings … it always came down to the fact that my father was a greedy, oily Coolie, and my mother was a Bushman, with twisted hair and twisted brains. Once the shouting was so loud, so raw and so angry that it frightened me more than any other occasion and I got in the middle of it.

I was sandwiched between my dad's generous belly and my mother's heaving chest. Begging for it to stop. I was horrified when I spotted a heavy pan of something hot in my mother's hands, petrified it would be launched at my father. I saw his fist start to form and knew it would land on a familiar part of my mother's face. I felt my lip tear and blood leap onto my father's sweater as I tried to use my body as a white flag to stop the war.

I don't remember how it ended but I do remember fear and fatigue and awful self-blame. Then the conversations I had with my dad when he came home from work every day started to make cold, clear sense. I thought he was being friendly, extra caring, when he invited me for a walk up the road to the shop. The prospect of treats on a weekday was exhilarating and I recall walking and skipping the way children do when they are about to be spoilt, my hands clasped in his warm, fatherly, doting grasp.

He would ask me ordinary questions like if my mum had gone out that day. If she had seen anyone or if anyone had come to the house. I answered blandly in that childlike way, distracted by the rare pleasure of a packet of chips and a cool-drink. Once we got home I'd watch him turn my innocent answers into deadly accusations that would escalate into the familiar loud, throbbing music of shouting and begging, crying, swearing and punching.

I don't remember where my older brother was that day but I do remember waking up one morning after a particularly bad fight and looking for my mum. She used to love wearing a favourite blue, floral dress and as there weren't too many places to look in that tight space, I flopped onto my parents' bed and peeped over the side closest to the wardrobes and there she was. Lying there. Still. Her dress soaked in blood, the flowers grotesquely obscured as if a child had finger painted over them, her face swollen.

I see it all so vividly as I write this ...

On a similar morning not long after this I was playing in the main house in the bedroom of one of our landlord's children when I parted the curtains after hearing a noise outside and saw the police arrive. We were not told why they were there. They did what they needed to and as they left an officer turned around and looked at me. His gaze caught mine and I am still haunted by the look he gave me and the words he mouthed. I thought I heard him blame me and I recoiled in terror, scared I was going to jail. But deeper than that was a fear turned inside out, into the fear of myself. Was I the reason for my father's anger and my mother's suffering? The question haunts me today, even though I know that to blame a child is to place an extraordinary and unfair burden on their psyche.

I could never ask my mum personal questions when we were little, suppressing them as they burnt and threatened to defect from my mouth into her ears. There was so much I needed, so much I wanted to know. Because for many of us who grew up in brown communities, children were never allowed to ask big people questions. We would be accused of being 'ougat'. Too big for our boots. There were conversations adults had and there was the playful chatter of children and an impenetrable, steel door bolted by convention and respect stood between the two.

'Don't stand there counting teeth!' an adult would shout, as we scurried out of lounges and sitting rooms where they congregated, artfully dodging a smack on the behind from the grown-up closest to us. So I could never ask my mother for absolution. I could never get her to confirm whether she thought I had any culpability in her suffering. It seems the answers were forever tucked behind the sutures of her wounds, silent and covered up. That to ask would rip and tear her scar tissue and lay bare all that pain once again. And so, like many families in our communities, we moved on. We gathered up our issues like cloaks around us, tightly girding pain and suffering, turning them into weapons we could use to insulate and defend us against future pain and suffering.

When I look at pictures of my early childhood, of birthday parties and smiling parents, I try to penetrate the spaces in-between for clues about unspoken silences. When I proudly show friends that treasured New Year's Eve party picture of my mum and dad where she looked like a film star and he, her dashing leading man, I wonder whether the smiles were genuine. Whether the gay projection was a cover-up for a private horror movie playing on a screen as invisible as my mum's pain and my father's guilt.

Sometimes we choose to look at things in a way that's shallow, in a way that doesn't excavate too much so we can remain insulated in our insistent belief that all is well. Welcome to Alternate Reality Town, folks, where like the preachers say, 'seeing you see not, hearing you hear not and neither do you understand'!

It was before my teens when the 'choose heaven or taste hell' sales pitch of an evangelist swayed my father and helped him 'find the Lord and be saved'. He was a totally changed man who seemed to genuinely and deeply regret the trauma he'd inflicted on my mother. I watched their affection grow towards each other and the only time I'd see him raise his hands after that was towards the sky, eyes closed, sincerely praising God for his salvation and singing hymns loudly but off-key. My dad both sang and danced on the side of the beat.

It was with him that we gathered around our bed every morning. On our knees, heads bowed and fingers clasped, we looked like those perfect but unreal pictures in the Jehovah's Witness magazines as we began to pray with his trademark trio of bellows, 'Hallelujah, hallelujah, hallelujah, heavenly father we …'

I never saw him raise his hand to Mummy again.

And so, along with the games and toys of childhood, I sealed in a large box the blood and violence of the Wounding Years. It helped me move on because I loved my father so deeply and was always searching for that special spot under his arm, beneath which I felt safe and protected from the world.

4

Aunty, you Want Brass?

The phone at house number nine would ring early on a Saturday morning. It would be my Aunty Eileen, my mother's sister, probing and laughing as she asked, 'Is your mom catching the dust?' My mum's penchant for shiny floors and a pristine house was a well-known joke in our family. Her sisters couldn't understand why the ritual of cleaning had to happen day after day, why cupboards had to be routinely straightened and organised and why the level of dust seemed to be directly proportionate to my mum's measure of self-worth and purpose. The more dust there was, the more reason to feel bad. I seem to have inherited that trait.

My aunties knew my mother's world would be off-kilter if there was even a light, almost mocking, powdering of dust visible on the brown wooden arms on the sides of the loud, florally couches of our semi-detached cinder-block house. 'Aunty Maureen likes a clean space,' they'd say. Cleanliness was next to godliness and my family worshipped every day; twice on Saturdays and Sundays!

On weekends my sister Jenny and I would be roused early. Like seven a.m. early – much to our irritation and whispered complaints. My older brother Eugene would typically be left to sleep a little longer, ensconced as he was in the protection of male privilege. We were firmly in the era of housework being a girl's domain so there was no time for resentment or revolution; we had work to do.

My mum was convinced that if the curtains and windows were not opened wide, we would choke on the smell of yesterday's feet and bums. 'Air the place out, let the wind blow through,' she would declare like a ship's captain corralling a snoozy crew and summoning the breeze. I think she got a special enjoyment out of seeing curtains billowing and fanning the house. It was like demonic, dirty spirits were being exorcised and banished through the liberal libations of cleaning fluid and wind.

My sister and I would roll out of bed, sleep still in our eyes, carefully peeling apart the eight-hour crust and you could forget about pulling off the stocking that was keeping our hair 'swirled' and pristine. Friday was the big wash-and-roller day so that come Saturday we'd be 'boning' (Durban slang for looking sharp) and ready to go out should the opportunity present itself. As a consequence the wretched pantyhose (invariably a torn pair that was of no use to my mum anymore) had to stay in place because God forbid the sweat crept in and made our hair 'go home'. Wherever that was. The grand clean-up usually meant that the illusion of straight hair would be compromised and endangered as we sweated so much it messed up our roots.

So we'd reluctantly get up, grabbing the trademark Durban grass brooms and sweeping furiously, almost feeling the imagined dust storm from the shaggy carpet making its way up and into the healthy geography of our lungs. Aunty Eileen was always worried that we were chasing the dust and that we would get dust emphysema. Not that I'm sure this is even possible.

Cushions were vigorously punched and 'refreshed' for a day of sofa posing; they were highly vulnerable to sweaty backs in the Durban humidity. I guess mum's saving grace was that at least she didn't let herself get sucked in by the latest trend of covering the couches in plastic. That would have been the ultimate insult (and a painful one) as your skin welded with the see-through stuff and released like duct tape being pulled off a kidnap victim's mouth.

This was a mania that washed over our community at the time in a bid to preserve, for as long as possible, the coveted New Furniture Look. The trouble was no one ever dared release those sofas from their suffocation, so the torn and tattered plastic remained in their arranged marriage through old age and then to the inevitable dumping on the side of the road.

It was always easy to tell when mum was 'dik' about something. Everything in her path would be cleaned violently. The choreography would be thus: epithet, punch cushion, epithet, wipe surface – hard – till her energy was then transferred to hapless ornaments and objects that refrained from back chatting.

The sanctifying cream of Handy Andy was laced liberally on counters and toilet seats. If we could have flossed the toilet, I'm sure we would have. Clean, clean and clean some more. Curtains were hitched up like Victorian skirts on muddy streets, twisted cruelly and stuck into the ornate burglar bars. The burglar bars were a real thing in the hood and ours were made up of pieces of metal 'shining' out of a half sun. The day the welder came to fit the bars our neighbours were so impressed they were wooed into commissioning a fancy design of their own, complete with Aum signs and fancy swirls.

Then, like in most Indian homes, the room divider took

pride of place and stared down at us; brown, high and full of shelves. Every spare inch of shelf real estate was occupied by a brass object. Brass cranes, brass baskets, brass pots, brass candelabra. Who knew that everything created on earth had its exact likeness in heavy, intricately designed and highly tarnishable brass?

If those objects weren't burnished to a shine that could challenge the superiority of actual gold, life wasn't worth living. We had to take each object down, apply lashings of Brasso, wait for it to dry and then rub them with a soft cloth till they looked proud and showy once more. It was a job we'd try to fob off on each other but for some reason I didn't mind doing it. I loved curating my mother's hoard of treasures and watching them transform from dull back to shiny.

The chair backs (the bane of my existence) that were draped over the backs of chairs and assaulted rugs (beaten spiritedly) were replaced on pristine floors and occasionally there'd be an insistent tapping on the window. Mum would go and investigate, pull the curtain aside and there would be a shady-looking man standing at the window.

I'll call him Selvanathan because I always thought that name suited him. He had tried his luck with my mum a few times. Selvas would stand at that window, lower his face and in a soft, conspiratorial tone say, 'Morning Aunty, you want brass?' Then he would open the front of his dubious, grimy windbreaker and produce several heavy items covered in handkerchiefs or newspaper. 'I got nice things for you, Ma, nice peacocks and all. Please 'elp me, the garners got no food at 'ome.'

My mother would look at him and ask, 'You sure this isn't stolen? Where you got these things from?' and Selvas and his gold slit would sheepishly answer, 'Nowhere Aunty, sathima, I'm selling my own things because I lost my job.'

While Selvas was telling my mother his story of woe and unemployment there would be another commotion making its way down the road. A loud hooting would bounce between the tightly packed houses in our small street, rattling windows with a cacophony of shrieks. It belonged to a rickety bakkie that was stacked high with cages, leaving tufts of feathers like a trail of pamphlets behind it as it drove down the street. Sticking their reddish beaks as far as they could beyond the chicken wire were real, live chickens. Actually, not chickens but fowls. 'Live fowls, live fowls!' Beep, beep, beep the hooter cried. 'Ninety rand for two! Fowl, fowl, fowl!'

It was Fowl Uncle! As the woeful cluckers stared their fate in the eye, our mothers picked the best as they gathered outside trying to bargain the uncle down, each vying with the other for the choicest, plumpest one.

Soon the selection was made, the money dispensed and before long, with one loud cluck and a wresting of feathers, the bird was drowned in boiling water and transformed into lunch. There is nothing quite like fowl curry, even the giblets and unlaid eggs would cook with the UTD (up-to-date) potatoes softening perfectly alongside. 'Gravy soakers' we called them. Your curry alchemy had to be just right otherwise it was proof you couldn't cook. There had to be enough spice, water and meat that you didn't have to dig for like virtue in a prison.

But I'm telling the story all wrong. Firstly, if anyone had trouble catching and killing their fowl the curry would be dubbed 'running fowl curry'. I used to cover my ears and pretend I couldn't hear the chicken's death shrieks as my mum expertly wrung its neck.

By lunchtime the weekend pageant was firmly in play. You'd open the pot lid to find steam escaping, then sprinkle a liberal layer of dhania on top and the curry was ready to serve. The house and occupants would be clean and shiny and the plates on the table. Plus a nice carrot salad (with just the right number of chillies), a chilled two-litre Coke and the perfect day was in the making.

My mother would frown on young girls who were still in their pyjamas at midday. An older woman who lived behind our house in the renting schemes was worse and took a dim view of the girls appearing in public later in the afternoon dolled up and preened. She would take one look at them and declare intolerantly, 'Look at those girls, the way they like to posh up in public, but their house is so dirty!' We would just laugh at her patent indignation.

But back to Fowl Uncle. If we didn't know an aunty or uncle's name (yes, everyone was respectfully called this) we just made one up. So the lady who was always carrying bags would be Packet Aunty. 'You know Packet Aunty got sick and they took her to Gandhi Hospital, so her high pressure went away!' and you'd know exactly who they were talking about. Or Samoosa Aunty, the aunty that lived a few streets away and who walked with a limp and a basket of goodies. She would cheerily pass by our house selling 'fresh, fresh samoosas'.

Everyone in the neighbourhood would joke about the mythical but dangerous characters called Bush Knife Bobby and his accomplices Rooks and Cooks from the Twos. You didn't want to get tangled up in a fight with any of them or you could be could playing out another scene from the theatre of township life, the classic 'hold-me-back' with its false sense of bravado.

It seemed no one really wanted to fight but needed to demonstrate a tentative bravery. Sometimes the fighting got real and if a young man didn't end up in hospital after being slashed in the face or stabbed with an Okapi, then he ended up dead on the street after a fight over some 'chick' or the unfortunate 'bumping' of another guy in a club or on the street.

Life in Phoenix was not just about what happened in a single house on a single street. Somehow our stories were all connected and interwoven with the lives and idiosyncrasies of our neighbours. Like that of the inimitable Aunty Maliga.

Aunty Mali was something; a real character. She had a big heart housed in a big body. She had chubby hands and her red nail polish shouted off her long, pointy nails. Her hair was long and like the style of many women in our neighbourhood, worn in a single plait that bounced off her generous back. Her tent-like dresses were more functional than stylish, and came in every colour God created, the brighter the better. Of course she had the obligatory gold slit that would sparkle as her stories were spun from a spindle dishing sauce and drama and her superpowers were her jokes and her smile.

She was the original community CSI and would sit at the top of a long flight of crudely formed concrete steps just outside her front door. It was from this vantage point that she watched life in the Thirteens roll by. The architects of our communities carved the area up into units. So Unit 13 was ours, Lenham, where all the street names ended with the suffix -len. Sorlen, Triplen, Dunlen. None of those names meant anything and bore no evidence of creativity or care; we were numbers to the authorities, it would seem.

Aunty Mali knew all the stories. She knew that our next-door neighbour's brother-in-law was shagging the woman that lived in the row of renting schemes just behind our home. She knew which families were struggling ('yesterday they came asking for tin fish,' she'd declare) and she knew which boys were sleeping with which girls. Anything you wanted to know, ask Mali.

Aunty Mali loved her crocheted dolls almost as much as my mum loved her brass. The dolls concealed under their voluminous, gaudy folds a secret toilet roll. They sat not only on the cistern but also on top of a cabinet in the lounge next to an army of porcelain houses and roosters.

Sitting on the steps in front of the house or even on the pavement is so authentic to township life. People sit and watch humanity pass by all day long, they greet and have conversations. When we bought our first home in Johannesburg our entertainment area was at the back of the house, with lovely chairs to sit on and a pool to cool your eyes. But no, every time I came home when my parents were visiting, they would gather up their deck chairs to make way for my car to take its spot in the driveway. I'd always say to them, 'But there's a whole backyard!' and they would laugh and look at me sheepishly. The backyard wasn't as delicious and rich in gossip as the front and they'd chat to the strangers walking by in an overfamiliar way while I cringed at the thought of people I did not know knowing our business.

In Phoenix it was worse because everybody knew everyone else and they were tight. Curry leaves would be shared under the shade of a cluster of flagged junda (religious bamboo) poles together with regular updates on community life. This was the age of the original Twitter and boy did some stories trend!

5

A Green Bakkie and a Biryani Pot

During the week the dark green bakkie that belonged to the shipping firm my father worked for complained under the industrial weight of port supplies and equipment. But on the weekend its open back was invaded by an assortment of children, adults and pots of food destined for the sandy dunes of Battery Beach One or Two (for the Coloureds) or Sunkist (for the Indians) because this was during apartheid, after all. Our family itself was a biryani of mixed races so the choice of which of these beaches to go to was determined purely by the volume of the hordes making camp and invading the shoreline.

It was a time when kids didn't have 'skaam cells' (shame and mortification) about riding in the open back where the whole neighbourhood could see you. These days children seem to be embarrassed by the tiniest things: 'The car is too old, don't drop me off in front of my friends'; 'Mom! Don't kiss me when you drop me off! Mom!'

It was also a time when it seemed parents had less fear and dread than they do today about children not wearing seat belts or about paedophiles roaming the neighbourhood preying on their little ones.

We used to play outside in the street until it was dark, jumping over old stockings and turning cartwheels, way too innocent to care about our panties showing. We'd get scolded and smacked on our arms or bottoms, whichever was closest, for delaying bath time and neglecting to do our homework or chores. As the favourite leather belt, wet dishcloth or naked palm connected with our skin we yelped and protested. The hot klaps were metronomically synchronised with shouts of, 'You. Will. Listen. I'm. Sick. Of. Your. Mouth.' Ah, the staccato of beating in the orchestra of punishment. And we were the drums. It never crossed our minds to challenge our mothers or fathers for hitting us. They were gods, we their creation and we knew we'd catch it if we got on their wrong side. Simple.

Once a year the green bakkie was woken up extra early.

It was the day of the main beach event of the year, the annual church picnic down the coast at a tidal pool called Park Rynie. It was a long, long trip (in reality it was only a 45-minute drive) so we'd get up when it was still dark, half-asleep and wearily help my father load all the gear we needed and enough food to feed five families.

We snuggled beneath the weight of blankets and pillows, squashed together as the pick-up of an extra cousin or aunty or uncle here and there severely rationed the space in the back. But we didn't mind. We were together and a day of glorious fun would be unveiled as the sun stretched its legs and prepared to wake up.

The urgency to get there was justified because a great parking space determined whether or not we would overlook a nice spot and be spared the marathon trek from Cairo to the shore, dangerously balancing gas stove, groceries, umbrellas, chairs and our big, black tube. The tube, harvested from a massive truck tyre, would later become the envy of all for its ability to lasso the waves that crashed over the tidal pool walls. We may have been paupers elsewhere but on the water we were royalty, baby!

The carefree romance of the moment was made even more special as the trusted gas stove roared into life, while my mother kneaded, balled and rolled dough. She magicked a swift procession of fresh, hot, delicious rotis that would faint off the picnic production line straight onto waiting paper plates. The smell of a fresh curry sent word across the beach, deploying my mother's emissaries of fragrantly uplifting curry leaves, curry powder, ginger and garlic which called out, 'Mutton curry, mutton curry, come one, come all!' And soon the brothers and sisters of Living Waters Church were Pied Pipered to the spot around Mum's pot of wonder for a taste of the glory. The satisfaction on my parents' faces told me they were happy and were proud of themselves.

As the rotis were filled, so too was the pool. Young girls with sinfully skimpy costumes took their time wading in, making sure the boys saw every 'accidental' bend and snap. Grandpas with grey chest hairs threw their grandchildren up into the air, and swept them across the water as shouts of glee threatened to disturb beds of mussels fast asleep in their shells against the tidal wall.

Our connection, or more accurately my obsession with the water, was deepened during these outings. I looked at the sea greedily, impatiently, lustily. I would start the beach ritual by massaging a handful of conditioner (the amazing Mediscalp in that bright yellow pot, remember?) into my curls. Its silky cream would indemnify me from the catastrophe of complex tangles and tear-wrenching knots in the bath later that night.

Then I would dive into the water desperately, as if it was going to disappear. When I was younger, I would spy my father far out away from the crowds that were treading water near the shore. It was almost as if he was jealous of the affection other people had for his element. He wanted a portion of it that was just his and he would signal for me to join him up front, even though I was so young. He knew I was a good swimmer. Self-taught, by the way, as my brother Eugene and I secretly imitated children and their instructors at the Asherville Pool on Saturdays. Admittedly I did almost drown once trying to dolphin-pod follow the other kids to the deep end.

My father always encouraged me to swim out further and transform my fear into power. And I still do, staying as far out as I can, for as long as I can. My cousin Karen, who I'm very close to, jokes about which ships I've seen and whether the shark nets that stretch along the coastline are in good condition.

It's in the amniotic fluid of the planet's womb, shut off, that I feel truly free and detached from everything that roots me to adulthood and responsibility. I appreciate the honesty of the waves as they buffet you, baptise you and wash you clean.

I sometimes wonder whether my affection for the ocean, rain or shine, rain especially, is because it is a way of holding on to Dad after all these years. That the reason I resist getting out is because I feel his spirit in the waves and I imagine he is calling out to me and reminding me of happy times. (Put in margin: book shrink appointment.)

These days spitefully prolific bumps of cellulite and wobbly tummy flaps (thanks kids) threaten to shame me out of my enjoyment of my element, but desire always wins and before I can even register disapproving faces I am neck deep in pure bliss.

Hours and hours later, skin wrinkled and roasted, the spell is broken by desperately shouted, urgent calls of 'Vaneeeesss-saaa! We're going home now Vaaaannneeeessaaaaa!'

6

Craving Wholeness

I have craved wholeness my whole life. Growing up I wanted everything and everyone to be in their place; it made my mind feel tidy. I always needed everyone together; an outing with just my mum or my dad made me feel anxious. The circle couldn't close if someone was missing. This settled into an unhealthy pathology that is still with me today.

I've described the toxic war that existed between our family and my dad's siblings. It was bad enough that they had felt some type of ownership and control over my father but it became even more insidious.

The price for brokering peace was the arrival of a

newborn baby boy.

At a time when a couple is meant to celebrate their first child together, I'm told my grandparents demanded my brother from my father. They arrived like militia at the family commune my parents shared with other young families in Sea Cow Lake. They rolled in in impressive black American-made, left-hand drive cars and took that baby from my parents. I have been told how my mother cried, how my dad protested but they were impotent to bring my brother back home; to let him suckle from my mother's breast, to raise him and build the bonds between child and parent.

Anthony, or Prakash as he was known in the district in Puntans Hill, would grow up at the feet of my Amma, living a lavish life as he was doted upon and feted. I don't know what other steps my parents could've taken but it seems they were defeated and thus relented to the wishes of my dad's powerful family.

So my brother Eugene (who came after Anthony) and I lived with my parents and we continued as if it was normal to have a sibling being raised elsewhere. We saw Anthony when we visited The Big House On The Hill and it was like we were from different families.

He was an enigma to us. He would pop up at various times, always wearing outrageously stylish or brand-new clothing that would make us marvel. He was a character;

loud, flamboyant and popular. His superpower was dancing and we often heard stories about how he would dazzle the crowds at some of the popular nightclubs liberally sprinkled around Durban, like Aromat on a stew. But more about that later. First, how we used to get into the city centre; a story all on its own.

If we wanted to go to the busy heart of town we often took one of the pimped-out buses that Phoenix was famous for. It would have something like a 'Lovers' Paradise' or a 'Reshma's Pride' screamingly emblazoned on the side and was painted in bright oranges and browns or blues and greens. The vast dashboard would be a cornucopia of stuffed bears and endlessly nodding dogs, presided overhead by big twin dice covered in red or blue towelling, dangling from the visor.

The back exterior of the bus was gaudily splayed with palm trees and broody beaches in an orange explosion of a sunset on some faraway island. Inside, one jostled for space, usually because the bus was full. One would try dodge a raised arm, especially if, as my mum complained, the person had a sponge of damp hair, ominously hovering above your head. If you could tolerate it, you could perch precariously on the steadily rising heat of the thinly carpeted engine area, till your bum couldn't take it anymore. The music felt like it came from the space behind your ribcage because of the force of the deep bass and, probably illegally, high decibels. There was a regular driver who seemed to have a special love for Clarence Carter's music and we'd be given an embarrassing, free lesson about lovemaking and passion as the explicit lyrics assaulted our ears.

We'd get off at the famous Beatrice Street ('Beetis Street, Ma') and walk the long distance to West Street with all its fancy shops. We'd open accounts at these shops and then pay off a dress or pair of shoes that we would wear for Eid, Diwali or Christmas. But mostly our store of choice would be the popular something-for-the-whole-family retailer called Ideals.

I would sometimes walk towards West Street to meet my mother after work, strutting down the working-class catwalk that was the Grey Street of the early nineties. The young salesmen tried to entice customers to *'gena phakathi,'* or 'come inside, very special prices' and were not shy to whistle at me and pay me compliments. I'd just go red in the face and smile shyly. If I ran into Anthony he would put his arm around me and those boys would be discouraged from looking at me, let alone 'charfing' me. They knew Anthony, often not just by his dancing reputation, but by his sometimes violent temper, and they knew they'd be in trouble if they dared show any interest in his baby sister.

In the end, these same streets took him. I learnt, while I was in Iran, that he was going to jail for a very serious crime. The news shocked me. I felt like I didn't really know him at all. And perhaps I didn't …

When I was growing up I harboured a precariously romantic idea of what our family was until little by little I was forced to modify the script. I wondered about the siblings that I didn't know even existed, that came in through the window when the front door of honesty was closed. Understandably, my parents were concerned about the judgement of neighbours and the perhaps overwhelming exercise of having to explain to us kids the complications of being an adult and the painful choices that went along with it.

One day my sister Jenny, who is five years older than me, appeared with hardly an explanation and we knew better than to ask. I made a decision to love her and to embrace her but childlike curiosity is a hard thing to suppress and it sometimes overwhelmed me at the worst of times. Once my mother was trying to divorce the strands of my tangled hair, roughly flaying them with a hard brush that brought tears to my eyes. It was a suicide mission to ask her anything at that precise moment but I decided to be brave.

I took a deep breath and courageously (foolishly) asked where Jenny had lived before she came to us. I got a stony stare as an answer. My mother's unspoken words were louder and more acidic than spoken ones. As she shot me a no-nonsense look, I looked down sheepishly at a latticed, green, plastic laundry bin piled high with her exotic shoes and stilettos and shut my mouth. My hair was oiled and plaited and I was released into the afternoon, forever closing the door on my question and suspending the inquest.

Then my older brother Leslie came into our lives when I drew close to my teens. He struggled to fit into a family routine long established without him. I felt for him and sensed his lack of belonging. I also felt for my father who seemed to struggle to give Leslie a chance and my pained mother who seemed to hope and pray all the pieces in our family puzzle would just fit and we could carry on whole and happy.

Leslie couldn't, or wouldn't, fit in. He was as recalcitrant as the impressive dreadlocks he grew later on in life. He would roll in and out of our lives. Years and years later he put down roots in a community of Rastafarians in a Cape Town settlement called Marcus Garvey succeeding, finally, in finding his peace and making a life for himself. It was tragic then that soon after he learnt about putting down roots, after so much upheaval in his life, death dragged him under allowing him the final boon of being able to breathe his last in my mother's arms.

It was during these times of change in my family, of deep personal change accompanied by the pain of disruption, that my resolve was sedimented to one day have a 'whole' family. There would be one father, one mother and their 'own' children and they would live in one house together and be 'normal'. As I grew older I met many other men and women who craved the same thing, only to find that across our communities this was about as possible as breathing indefinitely underwater.

My worst fears manifested when my own marriage was destroyed, slowly at first by the sniping beasts of betrayal, and then with lightning speed as an avalanche of names, dates and places brought the precarious edifice to its crumbling collapse. I was descending into the nightmare I'd sought immunity from. We were to be broken. Broken home. Broken children. Broken.

In the death of my marriage, the past was beginning to live again, bringing back old anxieties. It reduced to ash every hope I'd built up about love and security, about stability and about certainty. And the pain was excruciating and destructive. Pictures I had imagined about my future with children and a husband went up in flames. A time that should've been filled with shared joy about our children excelling at school, admonishing our girls about boys, sipping tea over talk about the day, had all been swept out with the tide. The picture of children with their own father and their own mother. Anything but a life of 'Meet Uncle So-and-So' or 'Aunty So-and-So'. A revolving door of people who would appear and disappear, confusing children into a distrust about adult relationships.

The betrayals made me detest close bonds with women,

whom I'd instinctively draw in as sisters. It almost totally annihilated my ability to believe that there are men who will mean what they say and follow through on that, who will speak plainly and respect my ability to deal with reality. Women, like me, are too often infantilised, too often 'protected for your own good'.

I know now that all the pretty pictures we paint over the course of our lives are illusions. A projection of what makes life whole and happy is just that, a pinhole allowing pre-chosen images to pass through but not the whole story. Reality is a holy place, a painful, perhaps brutal, but holy place. Living in it, speaking in its plain language can save time wasted on manufactured happiness and holographic feelings.

As I tried to reinvent myself and my idea of family in the post-marriage cold war, I had to become militant, defiant and tungsten-steel strong. I had to learn to make dinners and outings feel full. I learnt to cope alone with a sick child, driving myself to the hospital in the dead of night. I pored over budgets, making sure I could meet my children's needs. And I tried to find ways to keep laughing and having fun with my children, to find new things that make family, family. I still find it hard to be with other people when their children are present and mine aren't. I feel like I'm betraying them. I wonder, through their traumatic teenage years, whether I'm good enough as a mother in a context where I am sometimes made to feel like an outright failure. I kill myself trying to be everything for them; provider, counsellor and protector when the bad dreams wake them up. I do believe they deserve better than me but I have vowed to never stop trying for them.

The wholeness I've always craved has found an alternative form of expression. I am working with the version of my life that is right in front of me. I may not be enough, and our situation may not be perfect, but I'll die trying to give them everything.

7

Death Came at the Sink

I felt the first sting of death at the kitchen sink. It caught me, wrist deep in soapsuds in the stainless steel, single bowl washing dishes after school one day. 'Granny died.' As those two words hit my ears, squeezed from my mother's tight throat, I remember screaming. But in that displaced, faraway way, like it was coming from someone else. It was a strange feeling. Shock and incomprehension seemed to knock the wind out of my chest and flatten the small bubbles still playfully coming up for air from the silvery pool.

So this was what loss felt like.

The perfect security of the predictable always-been-here-always-will-be seemingly everlasting cast of the family album was cruelly altered by words. I learnt a different kind of science that day. The science that emotion, that intangible thing, had the power to change everything and was powerful enough to alter my reality. I would never see the world the same way again. I would actually have to make room for the possibility that the ones I loved the most would actually leave me and that it would feel really shit.

We went through the motions. I heard about a coffin having to be bought and the church having to be booked. There was bland discussion about who would cook the biryani, who would bring cake and how the tea would be served. Perhaps we humans need the rhythm and ritual of goodbyes and send-offs because it shows you a path to follow when you're a stranger in the land of mourning.

I overheard how my beloved grandmother was found, warm but lifeless in her bed, paramedics shaking their heads that it was too late to do anything to save her, as my Aunty Eileen pleaded with them to try everything.

I deciphered the real story of what death meant from the clues on my mother's face. Maureen wore a mantilla of stoicism for her sisters and her face was set in the stone of constancy. But I knew. I observed that her blank stares out of a window were actually moments in which a movie, only visible to her, was playing, showing her the past, with her mother the only actor, in graphic detail. She would grimace and tighten her mouth, as if doing so would prevent her distress from escaping.

I heard her cry softly, often triggered by random things. She'd be folding washing and her tears would give the T-shirts a second rinse. She would shake with an intensity that came from simple memories. Like the way her mother laughed in an unbridled and infectiously musical way. My mother endlessly mourned the loss of our granny, whom we fondly called Sisi.

I was to have an even more intense taste of loss years later. I was just sixteen and it was to be the second seismic event in my young life.

I begin the story on the anniversary of my father's death. It's the ninth of October. I look outside the window to the trees in the garden. The weather is noncommittal, undecided about whether to blow hot or cold. Unlike me. I'm certain that on that awful day many years ago, when the jagged teeth of pain sank deeply into my flesh, a part of me was lost. It's still missing from my being.

I'd just got off the phone with my mother. It's always a hard day no matter how many years have passed. Time heals all wounds? Ha! A handy thing to say when you have nothing sensible to say. But for those who have lost someone, you are always somehow right back there at the point of separation, through the cruelty of memory, where the edges are still sharp, the colours still stark and the feelings still raw.

No doubt my brother Eugene will call later in the day but we'll make light conversation about the anniversary, deliberate about not going too deep. We miss our father. Eugene is still hurting. And so am I. We both wanted our father to see us grown-up, with grandchildren he would have doted on. We wanted to be able to throw him the keys and let him drive the shiny new cars we were able to buy. We wanted him to be able to sit at a private table in a restaurant and order the finest cut of steak wearing a new coat and a fat, gold signet ring. We wanted him to be able to recline on a leather Lazy Boy and watch a TV so big, with pictures so crisp, it would have felt like he was in the India of his parents!

He'd be pained when as children we would creep along our neighbour's driveway, peering through a window trying to watch their TV. Or when we'd watch at another neighbour's house, whose children would make it clear that we were lucky to be experiencing such a privilege which was dependent on the whims of their generosity. We hated that but our desire to enjoy the novelty of moving pictures was stronger than humiliation. We managed to buy our own set years later but we never forgot how it felt to be made small.

Our father never got to see if we'd make it through life. He never saw the home improvements my brother made to the house he finally managed to buy for the family after waiting on a government list for years. The house came with a bathroom that had an actual bath (buckets had become so tedious, you know) and was tiled in pristine white squares. But most importantly it came with privacy as we had our own rooms. The day we moved in I wanted to lick the walls. I wanted to confirm it was all real. My mother quickly made sure we made the trek to 'our uncle in the furniture business' to buy our first ever bedroom suites, complete with wardrobes and dressing table. All on account, of course.

That was such a thing back then. Bedroom 'suites'. And a TV that sat boastfully in an actual room divider; another 'thing' back then.

I think my father would have beamed if he knew that I would be 'inside' the TV one day and that our surname would become familiar across the whole country! In your face Puntans Hill! (Just kidding)

But I have to go back, way back, to when a special bond between me and 'Punchas', as we'd sometimes tease him, began.

My mother tells me that on the day I was born it seemed as if my father was too. His light was switched on to maximum solar. She told me Daddy kept vigil at my bedside for the first few uncertain days outside my mother's womb. I was incredibly ill and an invasion of eczema marched across my body, angry and itchy. An ominous blue tinge stalked my eyelids and my lips behind the intravenous highways over my face, confirming my tenuous grip on life. My father haunted the corridors, pacing and worrying. He missed crucial days at work and didn't care if he lost the only job that kept our family fed and sheltered at the time. When I came home, Nirvana was made manifest. He doted on me. His baby girl.

My mother is so brutally candid (insert smile) about the fact that I 'was a miserable child'. A child who was demanding, not easily satisfied and determined to get exactly what she wanted. As I grew older, my nanny (who became that by default because she lived at the commune) was someone I became incredibly attached to and that I knew only as Nani. It was Nani who bore the brunt of my tantrums when I demanded French fries, perfectly cut and dotted meticulously with tomato sauce. I'm told I would thrash around and wail on the floor until my needs were met. (I think as an adult, I've become too polite about my desires.) And the angelic nature of Nani dictated that she would comply. Every time. Indulging the demon of a child that was me.

As I grew older, the story of my father and me was interwoven so beautifully into a tapestry of mutual admiration and affection. I craved his approval and would search his eyes for confirmation that I had done something well. I wanted to be the best at speeches and get the best marks for history projects and bring home trophies that he could admire. I left mathematics and science in Eugene's capable hands and together we made our parents proud that their children had shunned the street corner and were destined for a productive life. For a minute we were perfect. For a minute we were whole.

On Saturdays, after chores, I would shush my father's laughing protestations against me combing his hair. It was a ritual he would want to quickly get over and done with so that he could either do some shopping for my mother or go see his family but I always won. I'd grab a thin black comb and expertly style his hair. Parting it in the middle and slicking it down with the green grease of Kamillen Brilliantine 'For shiny hair', the choice of men with a certain middle-aged swag. Then I'd ruffle the top slightly to create the illusion of volume and he'd reward me with his generous smile of approval.

My father's belly was like a buffer; round and comforting. I knew that the space between his armpit and its curve would always offer me asylum. His hands were large, dark and squat, ridged with callouses. Those hands were powerful, as I learnt one unexpected night when I felt the force of one come down on my cheek.

I knew better but I could not keep my mouth shut during a loud row between him and my mother. As kids we knew when to back off when adults talked but I was a teenager and got too involved. I didn't listen so when my neck snapped to the side the shock registered on both our faces (it was the first time he'd ever struck me) and I looked at him with such contempt and vowed to never, ever forgive him. It took a lot for me to get over that and I think it was worse for him.

It wasn't too long after this incident when everything changed.

My father had just been promoted and came home in the blue overalls his new position of supervisor at the shipping company required. He'd flop onto his favourite couch and I would begin the ritual of taking off his heavy work boots, looking closely at the imprint of laces and grooves on his feet that stayed behind after I peeled off his socks. We'd make the usual jokes like 'Ooh Daddy, your feet stink!' and I'd hold my nose and scurry off to get a bowl of warm water. I'd wash his feet as my mother got his plate ready. As I worked up the suds into a lather, he'd look down at me and express his hopes for the better life he wanted us to have and for us not to have to work as hard as he did. 'An education my baby, you must get an education.'

If I'd known then that the end was so close, I would have gathered up every expression, every word, every action and stuffed them into a bottle and made an inventory so I would never forget. I'm frustrated by the spider webs spun by time that brush my face just as I can see the opaque outline of events, places and sayings. Before they can become sharper, more dimensional, they sprint through the maze of my memory and into the dark passage of forgetfulness. Gone. Just like that.

He got really sick really quickly. It was an unhappy throwback to the time, shortly after his diabetes diagnosis, when his tongue swelled, his eyes became like fat bulbs that almost exploded from their sockets and his sugar levels rose so high he nearly died.

But this time we didn't know what was wrong. He had sat in a chair overnight, too uncomfortable to sleep and Aunty Eileen was phoned early the next morning, hurried by Mum's panicked voice that screamed that something was terribly amiss. In the meantime a hospital bag was hastily packed and my father slipped on his favourite pair of blue-strapped beach thongs, as pain pulled his face into a tight grimace. Our hope was trained on Sydenham's Shifa Hospital. Shifa, meaning 'to heal'.

As Aunty Eileen appeared at the door we sprang up. Mum gathered my dad by his elbow and the intense shuffle towards the stairs communicated the pain he was in. I'm not sure he would have had a moment to consider the possibility that his leaving would be forever. As I watched helplessly, the dissociative numbness of denial was beginning to sedate my heart, which was totally unprepared for the possibility of my dad never sitting in that chair again.

As I began to lock up, the strange melancholy of an

opera poured out of the radio in my room, tapped at my ears and signalled for me to listen. I couldn't resist the message it wanted to give me, even in the middle of the chaos. I sat for a minute as the Italian words caressed the space between my face and the radio. The music rose and fell, profoundly affecting me and settling into the recesses of my psyche. I heard fleeting words that I did not understand but in them was a gift that remained. And I would be able to unwrap it, quite by accident, years later.

At Shifa, my dad was thrust into a confusing cycle of care but deteriorated steadily by late Saturday. On Sunday we moved him to a better hospital and an ICU that we prayed would fix him and return him to us. As my cousin and I mused that the fancy reception area of Parklands Hospital was like a home we'd like to live in in the future, my father made his final stand. I never thought, and still can't believe it's possible that someone so vital, so important, could just go like that. In a weekend.

As the hours dragged by, finally the nurses summoned us. Dad was losing his battle. The doctor whispered that they had done all they could and that my dad was ready to say goodbye. My brother Eugene and I shuffled into the ward. My father's breathing was laboured and his stomach rose and fell heavily. He spoke to both of us and said to me, 'Be a good girl, send your cousin in.' I hugged him and walked out as if I was in a dream and told Karen to go in. Minutes later the nurse nodded grimly to us and we knew it was over. The ground and my knees embraced, as finality slapped me hard across the face the same way his hand had done just months earlier.

Severe cognitive dissonance set in as I struggled to reconcile the picture of my dad when he was alive, laughing with him, washing his feet and combing his hair, the particular way he said 'my baby' and the person just metres away who had stopped breathing. I had never told my father I loved him. It was a message we preferred to demonstrate rather than articulate and I regret not feeling those words pass my lips and go into his soul, potentially nudging a smile from him.

To this day, when I think about him and say the word 'Daddy' a distinct pain settles between my ribs. How I have wished over the years for more time with him.

The funeral was a circus of suggestions that his family bury him in a traditional Telugu ceremony complete with a cremation, in exchange for a large sum of money. My mother resisted, defended by Eugene, who overnight had become the head of the home. And so the die was cast for a send-off that would rival the dramatic scenes that had been the soap opera of their relationship over the years.

On the day of my dad's funeral his body was brought home as was customary. Neighbours came to pay their respects as he lay in a casket in the backyard. My Amma held court over him; distraught and accusing. To her, my mother was to blame for her having to bear the burden of burying a child.

As I appeared at the kitchen door my grandmother looked at me and asked me, 'Why you didn't catch him Venesha? Why you didn't catch him when he was flying away?' It was hurtful then but it's funny now how our families' funerals can become the site of comedy and the outright ridiculous. Widows and widowers look down at the departed imploring, 'Who's gonna hold me now?' 'Why I made mutton curry when you asked me for fish curry?' But what was yet to unfold was to be no laughing matter.

Later that funeral morning, at the front of the sedate and quiet Living Waters Church, the organ poured its music over a substantial congregation of mourners. We sat in the first pew, me holding my mother's hand and all of us cried softly under black hats and head coverings. Then, all hell broke loose as my father's brothers and sisters rushed in, shouting and making a scene. I'm still not sure what the altercation was about but it had to do with accusations that my mother 'killed' my father and them demanding, again, that they be given my father's body to dispatch according to Hindu religious rites.

My brother Eugene naturally protested at the disruption, our other uncles and family friends stepped in, while my mother and I stared helplessly in horror. All that was missing was that toe-tapping banjo soundtrack that typically accompanies a saloon brawl in a Western. But instead of chairs being turned over and smashed my father's coffin almost was.

The Puntans Hill gang. No sense of decorum. As we say in Durban, they were 'acting raw'. Somehow the fracas was defused and we finally made it to Dad's spot at the Red Hill Cemetery.

Years later I was randomly switching between radio stations when I almost stopped breathing. An opera was playing that took me from my car on a street in Joburg back to my bedroom in Phoenix that morning my father left home forever. Pavarotti. Caruso. A song about goodbye that I didn't understand at the time that was so powerful it could sharpen memories and turn back time. A man saying goodbye to the one he loved; a message I adapted as if from my father to me. 'I love you very much; very, very much, you know; it is a chain by now that heats the blood inside the veins.' I wept.

8

The Sexual Revolution: The Back Story

The women in our sardine-packed communities regularly summoned each other to the kitchen door or front gate to commiserate, encourage, laugh, gossip, borrow a tin of fish or a fifty rand 'until Friday'. Many times their stories were a frayed tapestry of missed opportunities (Ey, I should have stayed in school), dreams deferred (I would have made a great lawyer), hard labour (God, this factory is killing my feet and breaking my back) and long-suffering (Lord, help me to not murder someone. I'm serious. Lord?).

But there was also a richness and depth that we were able to breathe in in very tight spaces. Because despite rarely or never having pampering spa days and manicures (Whaaaaaat? A fifty rand for nails? You must be playing!) their proximity to each other allowed the women to be real and to feel everything. The women I grew up with devised creative ways for their children to be entertained and for their families to be happy.

But others wore the exhausting and penny-stretching consequences of having children too early and putting down roots with men who were more tumbleweed than oak. This was before they wised up to the shallow guile of an opportunistic throw-up hastily executed as they walked down the street. Very rarely did what they eventually surrendered to behind closed doors, translate into happily-ever-afters and the comforting, clockwork regularity of bills being paid by dependable blue-collar sweat.

Stories would float into our ears like songs conjured up by a snake charmer, about men in the district who either didn't bring home money, or who were too busy gallivanting with this cherrie or that cherrie up the road and spoiling her with things that should be the obvious property of Aunty Saras or Aunty Cookie, who faithfully supported them no matter what. Those women still stayed despite knowing that the perfume he reeked of wasn't because of an accidental crop dusting at the Edgars perfume counter, but from an illicit love clinch as a result of boredom brought on by prolonged unemployment.

As a consequence, the ear-aching mantra of our aunts and neighbours was one of sacrificial lambs and martyrdom. It was about what they had given up to raise a family and how they, 'Had dreams you know of being someone!' But over bottles of red wine and limp wrists, made limp by the wine's defence-dropping influence, they hung futilely, clutching glasses that were in danger of crashing to the floor. Added to that, frequent melancholic doses of Judy 'If-I-could-be-in-two-places-at-the-same-time' Boucher and the fire and brimstone sermons rising sulphurously from the wet mouths of travelling evangelists under a massive, candy-striped tent down the street, they resolved that their girls would turn out better than they did. That they would not suffer. And the first defence would be the thrice daily ministration of the Gospel of Chastity. Amen.

Their convictions were deeply sedimented, having graduated summa cum laude as they did from The School Of Suffering (SOS). And suffering is an art form some of the women in our communities have perfected over many generations, it's almost a virtue. 'Red is your colour love but, wow, suffering really makes you pop!'

But on a serious note, while wiping away tears with the back of their wrists, they declared for their girls a life of power and prospects. And so it was with titanium resolve they sought to school us and prepare us for that most imminent of threats that came in the form of human sticks bearing arms and legs.

Boys. The packed full of wet dreams, hormone-raging, boiling blood-flooded teenage boys, who, much like the formidable bulldog ants who are notorious for stinging victims in quick succession and then injecting poison, were potentially deadly vessels of dream-destroying sperm.

The threat was made even more urgent by the fact that these 'marauders' had the power to Trojan horse their intentions by summoning butterflies and neutralising the defensive acid of sensibility. 'Attention Troops! Our girls need protection!'

Our mothers had to initiate us into the Grand Resistance, complete with the threat of orifice-invading plagues if we dared let the acne-covered enemy close enough to have 'just a little feel, how?'

They were brilliantly effective at embedding the fear of damnation into us. But even more terrifying to them was the prospect of shame. We were warned, alongside thoroughly brushing our teeth and wearing clean panties, that 'If you come home with a parcel, then that parcel is yours! Don't think I am bringing up another child, and in any case I'm too young to be a granny!' as they patted their hair and tried to pull in their bellies which, after having children, looked like folded laundry.

There was mourning of sackcloth and ash proportions if, despite all the social and pseudo-biological voodoo, you ended up 'pushing the wheelbarrow'.

Shame, they tried their best, teaching us how to weaponise our mouths and armourise our bodies in a war that as children we didn't fully understand but were prepared to blindly obey. Or at least try to …

And so no matter where a woman is in the world, whether Cape Town or Kabul, her mother's disapproving voice has the power to penetrate all physical barriers. It is a secret weapon all on its own, that sits penitently on the hard bench of experience in the front room of our conscience. From here it watches, wearing a disapproving or warning frown, knitting a judgement based on the decisions we make.

The Church of Chastity and Innocence was the first church we attended and whose totem was that finest and most fragile of tissues, The Hymen. All hail The Hymen! The preservation of this precious membrane was sacrosanct. So venerated was its intactness that it could be placed on an altar and worshipped. If you gave it away you were saying something about yourself. Something very bad.

We were warned to preserve it, to guard it like a special treasure that was to be opened only on the sacred bed of marriage by one's husband who would proudly verify that here was his prize, a chaste girl that was his to initiate into the mysteries of lovemaking. His property.

I'm convinced that the fatwas issued to us by our mothers

will live inside us until we die and are the invisible standards against which we measure ourselves.

So no matter what we did as teens, stealing kisses or having the odd 'vry' in a locker room, dorm or behind the school blocks (that left us sweaty and frustrated) we could hear their forbidding, clicking voices in our heads warning us to not let those boys 'pop your cherry'. And what we feared most was being labelled a 'loose girl', 'the village mattress' or a 'trampy trampoline'.

So with that being the background we came from, many only ever went so far with the boys, stopping short of threshold-crossing in our bid to not commit an undoable sin.

That one fragile membrane bore the burden and pressure of being the calculator of our value and purity. Across societies the measure of an unmarried girl or woman is predicated on its hallowed existence. Never mind that there are so many ways for it to tear and break without the help of a man.

But still 'the tighter the legs, the wider the gates of Heaven' was a war cry so strong that even as a liberal adult I confess to feeling a sense of psychic pollution and staining even when I know what I have done under the sheets is not a sin.

Their message, engineered partly out of religion and its attached severe and restrictive morality, has left behind a standard of behavioural hygiene that still, in some ways, calls the shots.

9

The Blunt Force Trauma of Love

I was thirteen. And puberty had hit harder than just the surprise of hair under my armpits, and elsewhere, that seemed to pitch a tent while I was sleeping. Puberty made my tummy hurt from more than just period pains. I was being assaulted by physical reactions coursing through my whole body that were more powerful than anything my necessary biological evolution had put me through thus far.

On a red stoep in dim light I would pretend to be sweeping but my eyes were trained on, no hypnotised by, the kitchen lights near the back door of the semi-detached house on the street above ours. I would catch myself forgetting to breathe as I scoured the doorpost for shadows cast or for the slightest movement. My whole universe seemed to have shrunk to encompass just the space between our stoep and that back door.

There was a boy who would appear from time to time like a spectre, a deliciously, fantasy-inducing, spectre that gave me my first lesson in 'the alternate scientific functions of the heart'. Yes, I learnt with grass broom in hand that one's heart can race and squeeze for reasons far more potent than just biological survival. I learnt that emotions, fever-like emotions, can give you a temperature, banish your hunger and render you useless while focusing on the movements of a single human being. Yes, okay, I admit that reading paperback romance novels about tortuously unsatisfying tales of a man and woman prevented from being together by disapproving family or circumstance, and finally requiting their love in a dramatic ending, did inform some of my expectations. The hastily finished books were always so achingly descriptive in their telling that I thought love had to be something so paradoxically painful but yet so worth it in the end. At times I would pragmatically dismiss those stories, reasoning that surely it couldn't be so difficult for those who were infected by real love to achieve the healing that came from being together. But nothing could have prepared me for my own initiation into the 'pangs'. They were so intoxicating that the very prospect of losing the object of one's affections had the power to send you to a gallows of your own creation, dangling from a sari's noose at the end of a mango tree. We often heard stories of young men, particularly, who were so distraught by a break-up that they took their own lives in a scene that could have come straight out of a Bollywood romance.

I can't recall how or when I started noticing the boy and realising that his strategic poses in the silhouette of a porch light were a signal that he was noticing me too. It led to a silly routine. I would endlessly sweep the stoep (kind of) and get shouted at, while he posed and looked down at me.

My mum would scold me, 'Vanessa, what are you still doing there, girl? Get inside now!' I would sigh and go back in the house pretending I was surprised at how late it was.

Soon the shadow in the door and I began to speak, inconspicuously, while his mother and mine cooked up schemes in their kitchens as to what to prepare for dinner as well as catching up on the latest gossip. While tins of bully beef were rolled open with their trademark keys and then thinly sliced and assembled with a slice of fresh tomato and a liberal sprinkling of salt and pepper, I munched carefully, barely tasting anything, deprived of an appetite when he was around. Sometimes I spoke incessantly, spitting out nonsense (and bully beef) in a vain attempt at deflecting attention away from my growing attraction to him.

But soon we became comfortable in each other's company and then it was normal for him to come down to our house and visit Jenny (who he'd also cemented a friendship with) and me. He would give me a hot smile that would transmit shards of enjoyment radiating from so deep inside that I thought I would faint and die on the spot. All the lectures and good old-fashioned wisdom that our mothers try to impart to us girls in their *How To Mould Good Girls* training manual doesn't prepare you for that first experience of infatuation (or love). It is the most unique and intense thing to have no knowledge of and to then know first-hand.

During these visits Jenny and I would sing gospel songs and keep him entertained. Until one night, when her back was turned, he planted a firm kiss on my lips. I thought I was going to cave into myself like a black hole. I felt dizzy and went to bed that night shivering and wondering how I would ever be normal around him again. His visits would increase as he served as pigeon carrier for dishes his mother cooked for us to taste.

The peck on my lips became more full-bodied. The hugs that accompanied them were like a charge; sending delightful frissons of energy all across the nerve network of my body. I noticed everything and I stored everything. Like at a joint family picnic that placed him alongside me and the brief graze of his hand along my thigh or the look in his eyes that became darker and more intense when he saw me. For my birthday he pushed into my hand a silver chain with his middle name, Leon, engraved on a pendant so that no one would guess it was from him. And I still can't listen to George Michael's *Careless Whisper* without thinking about that vinyl 'single' that accompanied the jewellery.

I took stock of everything about him like a pharmacist mixing a formulary. His commanding height, the curliness of his hair, the dimple in his cheek and his wolfish smile. We'd prolong a conversation, or even a silence, on the cement stairs leading down to my house, vowing that wherever we were in the world we'd look at the moon and conjure up each other. One night a shooting star sparkled across the sky and wishes were breathed under the moonlight for 'forever'.

I sound like those cheesy romance novels that I devoured but when you are young, your First Everything has a magnified intensity to it. It seems as if everything is etched indelibly in your soul and deeper than anything that comes after. The firsts are more colourful, fuller flavoured, higher and deeper. But along with the archiving of good memories, come memories that you'd rather forget but can't. These memories shape you and alter you forever.

Once the boy decided he could not hold his feelings in any longer he blurted them out to his mother, who told my mother, who told my strict father, who became incensed. His little girl, a teenager forbidden from even wearing lipstick was with a BOY! 'She's supposed to be focused on her books!' he raged. And despite the fact that we really were quite innocent, he interpreted our dalliance as a huge betrayal on my part and a dishonouring of our family.

A meeting was called between his parents and mine. The Montagues and Capulets of the Kingdom of Phoenix, circling in a duel of wills. The boy declared his feelings. I suppressed mine out of fear of my father's wrath. I saw something change in the boy and I knew something had changed in me too. Something had been irrevocably broken that night and as he slunk away, I crept into bed with my father's parting words, 'You said WHAT? That you LOVE him?!' like a finger pushing against my forehead.

And that is how it ended.

But feelings are like rivers, they flow around rocks and through crevices, determined to go on. And mine did. For a long time. I spent weeks crying dramatically on my best friend Meena's bed, two clicks shy of full-blown rending of garments and gnashing of teeth while she soothed my pain with words that were too weak to breach the surface of my stubborn ears.

The boy eventually went to the navy while I bled internally. He dated a close friend of mine, while I haemorrhaged some more, and then he made a girl pregnant and it was all over. It was my crucial initiation into how to pretend to not be affected. I even attended the shotgun wedding, dancing indifferently near the bride and groom's table, wearing the biggest, brightest smile and congratulating the happy couple, while all I wanted to do was break champagne glasses on the floor and wail in the shards while blood emptied out of my body like water through a colander. It is a defence I've perfected into an art form over the years that refuses, even on pain of death, to let the other person know he has hurt me. I dropped that mask only once, purely out of earth-shattering shock. And I will not do it again. The price of admitting one's devastation is too high and indifference seems to mitigate the blunt force trauma of being a loser in love.

10

Ai ...
those Brown Boys

One night my sister-friend Zahra (not her real name) and I were sitting on the deck at Johannesburg's Hyde Park Southern Sun. It was a beautiful spring evening and we were dressed to honour the full moon hovering above us watchfully. Zahra is beautiful; with thick, lush hair, curvy body and a killer dress sense finished off with leopard-print, red-soled Louboutins, which she arched to a halt under the table. And her top, well, it did little to conceal a glorious boob job. She turns heads.

The deck wasn't as choked as it can sometimes be and the night air was light and warm.

But the conversation was heavy. As the ice cubes in our glasses began to sweat and melt, we were transported to a time in our teens when the heat of puberty was strong and boys and girls were discovering that the tingles they felt had a purpose.

They were for stolen kisses under lemon trees, hearts fluttering, secret, smouldering looks exchanged while families greeted each other after church. They were for going to the corner shop for nothing at all just so the boy you liked could look at you and you could look at him. We were like squirrels, feasting on the tiniest nut of attention, making it last through wintery months hoping the dance would lead to a held hand or a first kiss.

This innocence, however, was growing and hardening into maturity under the cruel jackboot of apartheid and in the shadow of a time when one's value was predicated on the levels of your melanin. It was a system which was simply, and insidiously, brilliant.

It was evilly genius at not only alienating whole groups of people from each other (through the Group Areas Act, Immorality Act and others) but it toxically nurtured a particular type of self-loathing which ensured that not only would we be separate from each other and learn to hate each other (Black and White) but that the Blacks (Black, Indian, Coloured) would not even be able to look in the mirror and see self-worth doff its cap at the face staring back at it. We were programmed with a value system that made blackness the devil and whiteness virtuous. It made us like the parts of us that reflected whiteness and despise the parts that absorbed the sun, that browned and baked under the cursed sky of colonialism and repression.

Apartheid's architects made the beautiful, ugly. It made big bums and hips, kroes hair, full lips (the racists called them 'phuthu smackers') and browner, darker skin the attributes of ugliness. It made whiteness appear clean, special, perfectly shaped, 'fair and light' and a state to aspire to. We were in the church of social programming and the media at the time was our gospel.

It seems to me, and I only have environmental and anecdotal evidence to back this up so please feel free to have your own version, that it worked.

I remember looking into the mirror one day when I was a teenager. I put on the yellow denim skirt that my mother had bought me from the cheaper stores on Grey Street. I was perturbed that my bum stuck out, I hoped the tight skirt would hold it tightly and mould it into the pleasing, pancake-flat 'normal' of the women on the Jane Fonda videos and fitness bunnies on television, with their high-waisted leotards and neon tights that coated bodies with zero hips. I wore that skirt trying to suck in my tummy and the said rounded bottom as I sashayed to town with my mother, half-shy, half-confident. I laugh, in hindsight, because that would be the exact bum that would draw approving looks and a few numbers today!

I also sometimes dreamt of what it would be like to have naturally straight hair so I wouldn't have to face my Telugu Gran's admonition to oil it and plait it and grow it till it rivalled my cousin's envy-inducing, gloatingly thick plait.

For a while my brown skin bothered me ... until something changed. I reasoned. And what I saw made no sense. I stopped having my hair relaxed. I left the shallow waters of my self-loathing and began to really think. I can't say what catalysed it; perhaps it was the belated opportunity to mix with kids across the colour lines through a chance political camp encouraged by my history teacher; perhaps it was like snapping out of the reverie spun over my consciousness by living in a home where my parents feared any political talk. But whatever it was, finally, I began to see who I was and how much I was changed to love what was not me.

But allow me to take you to the church of my childhood for a moment.

Now, the Holy Spirit-filled Living Waters Full Gospel Church was interesting. When I was little it was still a wood and iron structure, with a tight congregation, where sometimes the band members doubled as ushers and collection takers and the services were small and intimate. You could even see the sweat roll off the faces of the pastors, so snugly fitted were the chairs.

Then the faithful grew and so did the tithes, until a fancy, double volume, airy hall, with proper wooden pews, big, light-beckoning windows, a resplendent red carpet rolled down a long aisle and a stage, offices and a kitchen were built alongside. It was here, atop the abundant, musky, red sand of Red Hill/Greenwood Park that the youth gathered for church for a special service every Friday night. They came from the area but also from outside where other 'Coloureds' lived.

The Coloured/brown/mixed-race/matisse/mulatto boys came from townships called Wentworth and were negatively stereotyped as follows: rough (read raw, might steek you), Newlands (similar), Greenwood Park (stervy, meaning stuck up and overly concerned with the state of their coif rather than the state of the world), Sydenham (also thought they shat ice cream and were shallow). At this, God's house, they would mingle with girls from the same areas, including the odd hybrid from Phoenix (me). Put all these ingredients together and very specific behaviour could be observed.

It was the straight-haired, light-skinned, read: 'fair' (eye roll), skinny (major eye roll), and preferably green or light-eyed chicks that could make the boys bib (jockey for attention).

In other words, they were 'God's Favourites (GFs)'.

You would overhear plans being laid on a Friday night about how this guy wanted to 'snipe' (kiss) that 'stekkie' (piece) and how she was so lukka (nice). But the camps were carefully demarcated between 'white-like specialness' and us lesser mortals. Read: my type: thickish body, wild, curly mop, brown skin and brown eyes. Well, we could have been lying on the floor breathing our last before one of the GFs would have had the decency or be bothered to cover us with a blanket so we could at least die warm.

Of course I'm exaggerating but you get the picture, right?

And yes, even the boys that were too 'Kurumanchi', as in looked like they came from Kuruman (the oasis of the Kalahari Desert in the Northern Cape), with their 'battling' hair (the type that didn't conform to aforementioned standards of acceptability) and darker skins suffered a similar fate of being relegated to the margins of anonymity. I had made peace with my lot and in any case the boys didn't really approach me because added to my 'undesirable' exterior, I came across as 'heavy' (too intense) or because I had an 'Intruders will be shot, survivors will be shot again' sign on my head.

I had too much of a 'mouth' as well as an overdose of cockiness so I was too much for their desire for a 'quick jam' (kiss). But I admit it stung sometimes, watching their interest in the GFs and not me or girls who looked like I did.

But back to the deck where Zahra and I clinked our glasses as shock wrote a reaction on my face to her story, uncannily similar to mine. At her school she was the bespectacled nerd with the recalcitrant mane of curls (her mother shunned relaxers), legs as straight as poles (not the coveted touch-in-only-two-places; ankles, calves. In other words, perfection). She also possessed the then shameful high bum and was therefore guaranteed not to crack a second look. When she confessed that, yes, she too was overlooked even though she was 'fair', I choked. And here I was saying how hot she is and she's telling me the boys didn't want her back then!

And nothing significant has changed except the boobs. Of course Zahra's fortunes have been boosted in a time where attitudes about women and their bodies have grown up and the fuller girl is ascending the throne. Now the men are panting for her chops.

I tried to understand where this all came from. And this isn't coming from someone who was vatted (slang for 'ignored') or jealous but as someone who just connected the dots in this way.

The girls in our church and in our communities were almost separated from each other by an unspoken checklist of value and worth imprinted on us after generations of living through class difference and genetic blessings and curses.

We only spoke about it in passing and jeeringly, 'Eh,

you know, so-and-so has got a lovely thread, she's a beautiful cherrie, I have to dallah that!' Or 'Ja, her ballie is up, they got span marcher.' (She has lovely hair, she's a beautiful girl, I have to get her. Her father has got a lot of money.)

The boys were also damaged and toxified by the programming of whiteness being the standard we were told to aspire to. Having a girl with the aforementioned blessings could be a currency of value they could trade in and be worth more than it was. If you showed up with a pretty girl, you were somebody.

What saddens me to this day, under a sky of freedom, at least outwardly, our men and women still carry the pathology of the past. That beneath their eyes, their desires are still defined by a rejection of themselves and the pursuit of worth that is the opposite of themselves.

It went a few layers deeper. I remember standing in that dubious space between the church and youthful adventure, feeling tested by their competing and contradictory pull. On Fridays after tech I would drink beers with friends at The Workshop, a popular student hang-out, or duck and dive to get to a nightclub (against my mum's wishes) on a Saturday night. I should have drunk more and observed less. Because it became increasingly, appallingly, apparent to me how 'Coloured' girls were fair prey for the local Muslim boys in many of these social settings.

Worse still were the boys that practically flew in for the weekend in their fancy sports cars revved to the max on the highway between Durban and Joburg (as they would loudly brag to anyone within earshot). They saw the sisters as easy meat. The girls saw them as 'nice-time' food and drink tickets or naively believed they'd be back to marry them. It was almost always a quid pro quo; my vagina for your wallet, my self-respect for your pleasure, and maybe somewhere in-between a miracle would happen where you'd see me, I'd see you and maybe there could be a future for us.

As usual, it was the GFs that were targeted first and months later you'd see them forlorn, broken, picking up the pieces of their hearts smashed against the lying mirror of a nightclub bathroom.

I saw this often. I hated it.

In Phoenix, I faced my own dilemma. 'Coloured' girls were for playing around with and mothers fretted their sons would end up with a girl like that. So boys played till they were 'fixed up' with someone more palatable, someone they could introduce to the family, someone his granny or older aunty would approve of. It was something I felt, not necessarily heard, but it was there. Some of the Indian boys I encountered perhaps expected that my legs would open like the doors of the local bakery and that my mouth would close like the coffin of my unfortunate neighbour's wife. That I was only worth the square centimetreage of my triangle. I still bear some of this resentment; I'm hypersensitive to being treated like I have no value or that I serve a purpose based only on what I can give to someone else. I crave being seen for having depth and intelligence more than anything else. It's silly and it's too much to expect from strangers who will never read the Book of I but it's there and perhaps I will get over it one day.

Again, my neither here nor there-ness cheated me out of a solid identity. I was Coloured in Unit 13 and Indian in Red Hill and each social setting amplified the stigma of not being completely enough or worthy of either. Indians and Coloureds busied themselves with looking down on each other and children like me were left to stare up at them lost in the middle.

As Zahra and I paid the bill and shared at last a hearty laugh over the past, I realised the chat had been cathartic. It allowed us to commiserate, it allowed us to name our triggers and it gave us the opportunity to celebrate the women we have become. Battle-scarred, a little mad, but real and open to still growing.

11

The Yellow Submarine

The well-salted fishermen at the end of Durban's North Pier were too absorbed in affixing bait to their hooks and shamelessly drinking beer in the morning, to notice the madrassa on wheels parked near the ankles of their body of concrete. While waves crashed against the rocks and drenched them in spray, there was a renewal and cleansing of a different kind taking place in earnest inside the curtained sanctuary of the Yellow Submarine. That was her nickname. Split-screened and proud, the old sunshine-coloured VW kombi was able to provide shelter, isolation and the choice to move, at a moment's notice, to a different location. It was a library, debating hall and university all in one. Books on comparative religion were scattered everywhere. I suppose this picture represented our minds in some ways, full of a thousand ideas, absorbed like water by a parched sponge.

I didn't know it then but the young man who owned her and was sharing this education by my side, would be the one I would later choose to join me on the journey of discovery and adventure. It's a funny story actually. The poor guy had asked me on a date and had hinted at wanting a relationship but I'd initially rejected his offer, affronted that he thought I was interested in the frivolity of romance. But later when I thought about it, I realised that we made sense and that we really were perfect for each other, given that we were both independent, brave and shared the passionate belief that we could not live like sheep following the herd. And so months after he asked me out, while employing the naughty trick of phone-tapping (my aunty had locked the phone to prevent us kids from doing exactly what I was doing), I called him and proposed. He was gobsmacked, appeared at my door in a hurry and accepted my offer of marriage.

But back to the pier. We were young and wild, roaming the savannah of the unknown, unafraid of the direction in which God would steer us. Our soundtrack was the rich, ebony depth of the legendary spiritual singer, Wintley Phipps. The submarine's speakers strained trying to contain his powerful baritone which carried us high above the soon-to-be fried fish and into the realm of the Lord himself. Even after our becoming Muslim, his voice would take us back to a time of Jesus belief and the soothing assurances of righteous reward. 'One more valley, one more river … one more mountain to cross, then I'll see Jesus in all of his glory … one more mountain and I'll be home.'

It was an odd contrast. The most provocative and potent of gospel singers providing the soundtrack to our journey down a path so alien to where we had started. There was such purity and honesty in those moments. The man I would go on to marry and I would debate with, to the point of surgical nausea, over every granular detail around divinity. We cared about the details; about achieving spiritual hygiene. Night would blend into day and still we'd be talking enthusiastically about spirituality and religion. Nothing else mattered. My world of volleyball and youth services, old friends and parties became smaller and smaller. It was just him and I. And it was perfect. If we were not in the sub, then we were on the Kawasaki 200 (trusted steed and future dowry), kitted out with side boxes like the ones from the American cop series, *Chips*, riding through The Valley of a Thousand Hills, picnicking by a roadside, revelling in nature. Always, always the talk was about God and how to achieve a holier, more elevated life.

We would go on to marry and debate and discussion were what defined us. We loved it and we shared it with strangers and friends. It was like the only language we knew. And we studied as much as we could.

But there was also a price for such exacting detail; the descent into obsessive observance, to the point of (to my mind) irrationality. And so light but painful cuts, like paper cuts, were starting to be inflicted on each other over sometimes incongruously ridiculous debates.

'Intense' can't describe what we were like as young people. When the search for 'truth' or perspective leaves the airy space of open debate and becomes claustrophobically restrictive and prescriptive, when it becomes intellectually violent or traumatising, when it ceases being a beautiful opening of a treasure trove of new ideas but the agent of repression, one must stop and consider.

We descended over time into a space I liken to a mind camp. Where slowly, equal partnership slides into dictatorship, where, unless with lawyer-like skills, you are able to defend what you believe to be a just position, you lose to the sheer dominance of an idea not so much rooted in rationality but in aggressive imposition 'or else'. The purity of listening and talking, speaking and being heard are lost. And where life should be an unbordered, open space, only a single, cold and concrete room remains and one person is in charge of the keys.

The mind camp. One of its early products was a piece of paper I found years after I left Islam and my marriage. A choke stuck a fist into my throat as a ruled sheet of paper that had as its heading, 'Reasons why you should not drive', fell out of a collection of belongings stored away. It was written as a contract, in the early days of conversion, which I was required to agree to and sign and contained about a dozen explanations as to why I shouldn't drive. In retrospect it was so basic, so silly and I can reject it now with contempt but not years earlier in the heat of endless debate, frustrated crying, pleading, stress and anxiety as I protested, and defended, my rights. I recall feeling so angry and helpless that I wanted to beat my breast and tear my hair out. Are we even debating this? It seems crazy. The mind camp. In which I was imprisoning myself. In which I receded more and more into myself, perhaps madly believing that by doing so I could just disappear and at the very least be free of the need to utter one single word more.

I have this palpable recollection of the sounds of the invisible chains of submission clicking and locking down different parts of me, a plastic wrapping squealing as it coiled itself around me, long, thick nails hammered into my tongue and sealing it to the roof of my mouth, thoughts viciously pulled back just millimetres away from the sky of freedom, lead poured into every available space, my being made silent and boarded up. This was a place a long, long way from the innocence of the submarine and its healthy debate. This was a place that was barren and joyless.

It hinted ominously at the future that was to come.

12

The I Do's and I Don'ts

The morning of my wedding arrived, covered in the light, trademark orangey mist of a Durban sunrise. As the colours began to braise the sky I felt reassured that the weather would be by my side even though my father couldn't. But just like my dad it abandoned me through season and circumstance. It was winter and there was a light coldness in the atmosphere that was hard to shake off while the clouds selfishly blocked the sun's countenance.

Like a spectre I moved absent-mindedly through the wood-and-iron rented house that we lived in at the time. I gathered up the things we would need that day, reaching into an old wardrobe and putting aside my fiancé's blue suit, recycled from some or other function. It barely fitted as the cuffs recoiled from his wrists and the pants screeched to a halt a noticeable distance from his ankles. Ankle-fighters, we would jokingly call them in Durban. Next to it I placed my graduation outfit, which I'd worn some months earlier. Black skirt, white shirt, odd multicoloured waistcoat and Florence Nightingale-style pumps. Oh and a random head scarf. Ordinary. Unspecial.

Just a few kilometres down the road from the house, my father would never have guessed the things that were going through my head and heart. His grave is near the entrance to Red Hill Cemetery beneath a tombstone bearing his long Telugu name, Panchavaranam Appana John Bull Rappetti. The red sand, which served as a barrier between his modest coffin and the blue-grey gravelly outer topping of the grave, kept secret from me any wisdom he might have whispered for me to the wind.

I thought about him fleetingly that day. The day he should have been walking me down the aisle. 'But what difference would it have made?' I asked the sparsely furnished room resignedly. Here I was, about to have a wedding like no one else in my family before. A wedding he surely would never have approved of had he still been alive because he would have said I would be betraying Jesus. Jesus who had turned his hard, heavy fists into soft hands that could finally be held gently against my mother's face.

There was to be no long, white dress and a flower-lavished aisle. No *Here Comes the Bride* enthusiastically played by a blue-rinsed, chignon-wearing, elderly lady perched in front of an old church piano. No fawning faces watching proudly and commenting approvingly over a lace dress with a breathtakingly long train. No cute flower girls and cherub-faced pageboys or best men and bridesmaids flirting surreptitiously. No confetti. No wild clapping and congratulations and no bestowing of hundreds of overly eager kisses outside the church.

I didn't care that there was not to be a feast for hundreds. I didn't care that there would be no presents because I was always somewhere else these days. Somewhere higher up. Higher than the minaret of the Queen Street Jumma Masjid. I stop there.

I turn my attention to the mundane rituals that must be done before what I really want to happen can begin. I gather together the secret weapons every woman, who has not been blessed with 'a good thread', has in her arsenal. I place on the dining room table an old, stained towel, plastic combs and rollers ranging from the trademark, highly favoured, tiny pink ones for tight, short curls to the larger, standard green ones for the longer bits of hair that have not broken off. Then an assortment of plastic torture pins are placed by the handful into a cup for easy deployment.

Woe betide your forehead if the first roller has a pin securing it that sinks into the skin near your hairline. You will spend wasted hours trying to massage away that singular, deep, telltale groove. The last thing you want people to think is that you actually have to roll your hair. No! You want them to believe that you woke up like that, elegantly and regally arising from your pillow and that your thread was just naturally heavenly straight and lush, without help from anything other than God blessing you with *gladdes*. (Durban slang for good hair)

Next I set down the final ingredient; the obligatory heavy plastic pot of relaxer. Relaxer. Never has there been a name for a product that does anything but make your hair relax. It burns your scalp. It stinks like the vapour of a hundred sulphuric experiments that went wrong and burnt down the lab. Relaxer cuts. It breaks. It sizzles. The only effect that's missing is smoke and sirens. Make sure you have cold, soothing water on tap.

The word 'relaxer' also seems to imply something else. Like your hair has been what? Uptight? Cross? Stervy? What it should be called is 'Surrender' because that is what women have been doing with their hair since the potion landed on supermarket shelves and in salons on the high and underground streets. Surrender to the stink and burn but emerge to the celestial harps and envious choruses of 'My, how wonderfully sleek and beautiful your hair is!'

By the way, I have an aunt in my extended family whose husband still believes her hair is naturally straight. The poor man is oblivious to the secret six-weekly visits to a stylist where the hot ooze of yellow and black straightening tubes is generously applied to slick the curl and calm the kroes roots. They have been married for thirty years and he still does not know what it takes to get his beloved wife to look more Indian and less Coloured. So I wonder what happens at night when she whips out the swirl *kous* and wraps it tightly around her head?

'Ready Vanessa?' my future mother-in-law, Celia, calls out, still insisting on using the name she met me with and resisting any talk of either Iman or Isa (her son and who she'd named Earl). She brings me back to the task at hand.

As I beat her tight curls into coherence, magicking a style from her resistant hair, my future mother-in-law is oblivious to the coils tightening around my own heart. I had to be stoic. What I was doing didn't bear the smiling approval of my mother or my extended family (who still didn't know that I was about to be married). My friends in the church were still dealing with the wounds of my 'betrayal' and anyway I had severed ties with anyone who disrespected my decision to become Muslim and get married on a Thursday in June. They were left on the ideological battlefield, defeated in their insistent attempts to 'win me back'.

As the relaxer prepared for a battle of its own with Celia's hair, I was winning the war against any residual angst I may have had about standing up for myself and following my own conscience.

Isa, Celia and I got dressed and piled into the car on loan from my future father-in-law. Following an obligatory puff of smoke from its ageing insides, we headed to the magistrate's court, making a single stop to pick up Isa's Granny Margaret who had been, by contrast with the rest of our families, a rather jolly witness to our journey.

Weddings and murders can never go unreported for long and lo and behold when we arrived at the court I saw that somehow word had crept out and 'surprise, surprise' my beloved cousin, Karen, and my two special aunties, Eileen and Alice, were waiting at the court, standing with my mother, having been tipped off about our plans. They didn't look happy. In fact I remember thinking the mood was distinctly funereal with their long faces and an apron of tears poised at the frontline of their eyes. But my heart leapt. Family would be there after all! Not my brothers, sister or best friends but at least some of the ones I loved most in the world would bear witness to the commitment I was making to a man I loved.

I realise now that I have my own children how hurtful my decision was; to charge forward and leave my family behind. There should have been time to try help them understand why my journey was unfolding in the way that it was. I should have waited a little longer. But youth and impetuosity are like a pair of shoes; inseparable. If my own children choose to leave me out of their most significant decisions one day, I suspect I will be devastated.

The inside of the court on that overcast afternoon reminded me of an Arab souk. Busy and loud; couples delirious with anticipation, uttering the marriage creed that has been used for generations to seal their love, having already haggled the T's and C's of their unions. A flurry of 'I do's' were exchanged and soon it was our turn. As I swivelled around to look at my witnesses, still their incongruously sad faces stared back. As if in a dream I heard myself say, 'I do!' and then laughed loudly and hysterically. I still don't know why I reacted in such a silly way, perhaps it was the nerves. But I looked up at Isa and all I needed were his facial reassurances and his tall, unspoken strength confirming that we were doing the right thing.

Today I look at the picture taken outside court and it certainly doesn't fit the style typical of wedding photos with bride and groom poses that usually embarrass the wedding albums themselves. We had one photo made up of a small group of people all with long faces, and the only smiles, I mean genuine smiles, came from the newlyweds.

We got back into the car, with my mother and granny this time, and my aunts and cousin went their own way. It was time for what Isa and I considered the real marriage ceremony.

We arrived at our favourite mosque with its yellow paint and gold domes and always noisy traffic speeding up Queen Street towards the highway. It was where Isa had been conducting tours and teaching visitors about Islam. Across the street is the IPCI, the propagation centre started by the famous Ahmad Deedat for the purpose of demolishing Christianity and offering Islam in its place. Deedat himself was waiting in his spacious office to offer some joy and affirmation to our day, a day that had been so joyless and sad so far.

My mum and Isa's granny were like a pair of mules, obstinate in their refusal to come upstairs to hear the Arabic words that would put the most important stamp on our marriage. Isa's granny remarked, 'What katla wedding is this?' Using the local slang which meant 'cheap'. I know my mum thought she'd be possessed and infected if she set foot in any religious space that was not a Christian one so instead she chose the spiritual safety of the car's back seat. As we walked away I saw her shake her head disapprovingly. I remember feeling amused but also sad that she couldn't put her feelings aside for one day and support us.

THE I DO'S AND I DON'TS

As we left them grumbling about 'what the hell kind of wedding this was' we headed upstairs and into the imam's office. Finally this was the portion of this whole saga we actually wanted to be a part of. The secular ceremony was about getting things right with the state but this was about getting things right with God. We sat in the office of Mohammed Sayed, who wore an unusually high white kufia (hat) and a white kurta (dress). His tiny frame looked like it was about to be swallowed by the flowing white robe.

He walked us through the marriage contract, covering things, which in retrospect I should have been paying attention to, like obligations and responsibilities and what would happen if, and when, there were other wives. I really should have listened closely because this would all become important later on. But at the time these questions of the flesh were vexatious to me. I was more interested in fulfilling the spiritual mandate of the faith and found the practical laws just necessary boxes to be ticked.

Then it came time to declare the dowry. We were young, and not of any means at all, so the silver Kawasaki 200 that had carried us on most of our journey through the transition from Christianity to Islam, served as the wedding gift. Of course it wasn't actually mine for long as we had to sell it to pay for the advance on the rent for the modest flat we took at the Good Hope Centre in Queen Street, not far from the mosque.

After the ritual we were called into Deedat's office. He had an envelope for us with a nice sum of money in it and he told us how proud he was of us. It was that money that paid for dinner for us and a few other friends that night who'd heard we'd got married. The dinner ended early. We said goodbye and then it was time to go home. And be married.

I remember it raining as night pulled its duvet over a dramatic and emotional day. I felt a brief flash of fear that I had done one more thing that was not done in my family. Part of me was happy and affirmed by the decisions I'd made but a part of me, the girl Vanessa, was afraid and feeling lost. Almost everything she was was being replaced by something else, by someone else. She was not to be seen again till many years later.

13

Of Prayer Mats, Head Coverings and Breaking up Family

Durban's Queen Street seemed to be something out of an exotic storybook à la the scenes conjured up in *Aladdin*. Its heart throbbed loudly as hooters screamed, competing with the ubiquitous, melodic sounds of the Muaddhin's call to prayer, as cars and people, trolleys and motorbikes precariously dodged each other, paying little attention to the exasperated traffic lights intended to keep everyone safe and in their place.

Many family-owned businesses, from clothing, jewellery and food shops, offered everything from stuffy, hot, three-piece suits for little boys to breathtaking, intricately designed

Indian gold jewellery for brides-to-be. The chokers, earrings and bangles twinkled so provocatively that it didn't surprise me they were so coveted.

The sweet shops seduced passers-by with their aromatic gulab jamuns sprinkled with coconut, perched on wide, flashy aluminium plates near front windows, while orange jalebi, in their spiralling circles, wanted nothing more than to belly dance onto an appreciative tongue and disappear to the sounds of a thrilled moan.

As the Adhaan seeped through loudspeakers and onto the street, it grabbed the faithful, who hastened to peel off their shoes, roll up their sleeves and prepare for the ritual wash, the wudhu, which would cleanse them physically and psychologically in preparation for prayer. Even the ablutions were worship, a sincere preparation for the ritual that turned the faces of the faithful towards Mecca and their hearts towards God.

'Hayah Alas Salah, Hayah Alal Fallah' (Hasten to prayer, hasten to success) the Arabic words extolled, as some men in robes and others in Western wear filed towards the entrance of the mosque.

I watched the congregation gathering from an office window just across the street, before taking up position on my own velvety red, richly designed musallah. I wanted to pray at the mosque and I was allowed access to the women's section but it didn't seem to be common practice for women to arrive in significant numbers. I discovered later on that in some places women preferred not to pray at the mosque, although there was no law preventing them from doing so. Indeed, it seemed generally accepted for women to stay away.

I was new to all of this. I was not quite strong enough nor did I want to stand out by going down to the masjid to own my space on the green carpet above the area where the men were beginning to line up behind the imam.

As I began, 'In the name of God …' I thought about the first time I prayed and the first time I drew a scarf over my head.

I had been discussing the philosophy of Islam at length with a religious teacher, firing off hundreds of questions that were answered, debated and challenged. I was far more concerned with the philosophical ideas, such as the concept of God, destiny and free will, than with the practical laws such as those governing dress. I had some issues with the notion of head coverings and why they were mandatory.

A lot of the given 'reasons' seemed to be more about the unbearable threat of provoking sin in a man (seduction) and by extension society (breaking up families), coupled with striving for a social purity too heavily dependent on the conduct of a woman than anything else.

But I was too impatient to delve deeper. Besides, I was

more concerned with the meaning of life, who the Creator was and how we should live morally rather than practically, to worry about cover or no cover.

I also relied on the work being done by Islamic feminists globally and by some vocal, local sisters I'd heard about, to venture into a battle they understood far better than me. I decided to listen to and engage with their points of view before I raised too much of a protest.

This might be a good time to share some light-hearted jokes about the politics of scarf-wearing. As a rule, no hair should be showing; so dangerous and powerful was each strand. Here is a sample ...

The Convertible: This scarf starts out by being appointed as a sentry and corralling every strand of hair. It sits close to the forehead in a pleasing and law-abiding way. But as the day progresses, and the further from view an imam or snitchy family member is, the further back it recedes until it is almost off the head. These women are constantly pulling up the scarf and setting it straight, which lasts only a few minutes until, again, it needs readjusting. And so it goes, up and down, just like the soft top of a convertible sports car.

The Cliffhanger: This style of wearing a scarf is a feat of science and achieves perfect balance. No one quite knows how she does it but the scarf is always precariously poised just centimetres shy of totally falling off but it doesn't and seems able to stay fixed somewhere between the hair's equator and neck. A box is ticked, the cloth is somewhere in the region it needs to be and its wearer narrowly escapes censure. Of course, you couldn't try this in a country such as Iran, where the religious police, à la the Brown Shirts or Basiji will look at you disapprovingly or even issue a stern warning that you desist.

The 'As God Willed It': This scarf is perfectly tucked in, preferably black, so that it doesn't draw attention with any loud, show-offey colours and is just the right blend of modesty and anonymity. It never needs adjusting and is generally secured in place with a pin. Good girl!

The Houdini: This type of scarf is hastily stowed in a backpack or bag the minute anyone who matters is out of sight, ready to be whipped out and put back on when the 'outing' is over and it's time to return to the places where wearing one matters.

And then there is The Eyes Have It: Needless to say, this is the head-to-toe covering that gives no hint of its owner except for her eyes. It's powerful and no-nonsense in its approach. You don't make eye contact and its wearer generally operates like a spectre in society, expertly driving cars and managing curious children. But no one dares engage with her except other women and females of the faith or the husband and family who know her identity.

But jokes aside, I had a serious choice to make. A choice that would make the change I had been talking about both visual and visceral for my peers and my family.

Finally, the day arrived when I decided it was time to outwardly wear the faith I had been discovering inwardly for months. I started my expedition in Queen Street and then found myself rounding the corner onto Grey Street where there was an abundance of shops selling all manner of coverings. There were the black Arabic abayas, the all-in-one, head-to-toe, penguin-like coverings. Some with long zippers down the front that came only in black. Then there were the burqas. These were not like the Afghani ones with full-netted face coverings but were comprised of separate pieces of cloth; a large tent-like top that had an open-face covering that flowed down to the waist area and you would then wear a dress underneath. There were niqabs; face veils, again, only in black, in all shapes and sizes and finally there were black or white gloves for concealing your hands.

I opted for the more unusual white burqa, worn with a white dress underneath. Plain cotton. Cheap. Nondescript. I really didn't care about achieving any particular look, I just wanted to make sure I was covered right and that I didn't look showy or flashy. This way of dressing was quite unusual, even in the community, where women generally wore Western clothing with a headscarf. I could almost hear them admonishing me; 'One can be fashionable and modest, you know!'

Fashion was the least of my concerns. I cared only that I was covered. I got over the embarrassment of not fitting in with the crowd and the strangeness I felt. I knew I must have looked a mess but again I didn't care. All this was happening against the backdrop of wanting to immerse myself, heart and soul, mind and body into the faith I was drinking like Zamzam water (holy water that comes from a holy well in Mecca).

I felt the most inexplicable feeling putting on that hijab. So much about my transition was about letting go. The devil-may-care girl that I was, the barefoot-walking, stranger-greeting, staying spontaneously in strange places, weird hairstyle experimentalist, torn jean-wearing, heart-open person was going inside and cutting myself off from almost everything that defined me before I accepted the creed and mouthed the words sealing my new pact, 'There is no god but God and Muhammad is his messenger.'

The trouble was that I had a family who at every step was struggling to accept and understand my decision. They had always thought of me as the wild one, the one that like a wild horse could not be tamed. The one of whom great things were expected. They were not ready for, nor did they expect me to embrace Islam, and seeing me in a covering, visually blocking me from them was a monumental event.

'But why Vanessa?' was the common, exasperated question they asked on repeat in the early days, 'Why?!'

When I answered, rather too militantly, that they just could not understand, it was like I was speaking another language. Then came the other changes. I couldn't eat with them because the food wasn't halaal. I couldn't be in their homes because some of them kept alcohol. I couldn't hug my male cousins, who were like brothers to me, because I could potentially marry them according to Islamic provisions. Some wouldn't let me pray in their homes because in their bornagain minds this religion was 'from the devil'. I couldn't pray with them in the way that I had since I was a child because I no longer believed as they did.

This was too much. But then I also changed my name. This was the last straw for my brother Eugene, Aunty Eileen and Aunty Alice and, of course, my mother. 'Whaaat? We must call you what? Iman? But why?'

I didn't win that battle then and I certainly haven't won it now. My entire family still calls me Vanessa. In the beginning it angered me. I could not understand, nor accept, that they refused to understand or accept me. The anger receded into hurt and then resignation but I'm over it now. And actually, it feels good to hear them say it.

The other question I got asked a lot at the time was, 'Aren't you hot in that thing?' Look, it was Durban; humid and sticky, even in winter, but the intriguing thing about faith is that when you believe as sincerely and fervently as I did the weather means nothing. I can truly say that while wearing a burqa or chador (the even 'hotter' garb that I threw on later) I never once thought about or experienced any discomfort. There was a joy that was steady and profound and simply impervious to the weather.

I wore the dress as worship. The simpler and the cheaper, the better. I now belonged to a universal group of people. As the layers descended so did my gaze. I lowered it. I shunned eye contact with males. I created boundaries.

In hindsight, with all the criticism that I hear about women who choose to wear coverings, some of which I now agree with quite passionately, it makes me have more empathy and more understanding for those who embrace the layers willingly, who do so not for convention or for their husbands but for themselves. There can be a regality about wearing coverings.

It would have been astounding to me to even consider shunning the hijab at the height of my belief but I owe you the confession of my thinking today, that it is anachronistic, has no relevance and in some places is an obvious flag and symbol of repression.

14

Going, Going, Gone!

The family of sounds spiritually swirling like dervishes towards the bedroom floor were so soft. They were a gentle whirring, a whispered tearing, followed by a snowflake-like falling. Clippings of downy hair were fainting into a Pick n Pay packet. As each follicle was cut it was like a child having its head drawn backward during baptism, steadily uprooted by the hunger of a pair of white, Wahl shears. Down the clumps fell, as lines that looked like tracks began to criss-cross my head. There was no time for formal goodbyes. Just a hasty surrender as nakedness marched into the spaces where clips and Alice bands once had a place to stay.

I looked up at myself. Not just a flick of the eyes but a real look. The eyes that burnt back at me through the mirror's truth didn't seem to even be in that room. They seemed to be, as they always did lately, somewhere higher up or deeper inside, depending on where you define the place you believe God is. I had just become a revert. Not a convert, as the imams sombrely reminded me. When you revert, you return to what you always were, a being in a state of submission to God. And so finding my way to Islam was, according to their beliefs, finding my way back to my original state.

Hair had become unnecessary to me. It became a hindrance. It wasted the time I wanted to spend on the more 'serious' aspects of my faith. Having to wash, comb, style and then tuck the hair under a headscarf and then run the risk of it peeping out like curious children from behind the white or black veil of my choosing, seemed so unimportant. No. I didn't want that. I wanted nothing to take my eyes off the book that was my oxygen and my reason for living.

A woman's crown was not majesty and beauty as I and society had previously conspired to legitimate. I was realising that if my body was transport for the soul, as someone once wrote, then my transport needed to be stripped down and bare. It would be free of the showy, attention-seeking stuff of coifs and colour.

Behind the white bedroom door of our commune I was

being born. I could have drawn an actual line in the sand that separated the moments after my new consciousness and the lifetime before with all the external lifestyle changes we were making. But it would not have shouted as loudly as engraving it so personally on my head.

The packet grew full. My head felt cold. I felt a dam rising within. I wanted to cry and laugh at the same time. I stood between two things: a previously open, liberal and carefree life and a new one of insularity, constant prayer and ritual.

What is it about hair that is so spiritual? Its power as a tool of adornment, adoration and aspiration is well-documented across the world's cultures but that night I could not equate the separation of my hair from my head with anything but the most powerful desire to take a stand.

Perhaps it's easier to fight a revolution through one's own body than it is in society. Or maybe the significance of conquering oneself gives rise to externalising the fight for whatever it is you believe in. What I was doing felt perfect. It felt like the more I could diminish myself and the vain trappings of being me, the more I could open myself up to worship and surrender.

It took me back to another moment in a new flat, months after we'd taken the first sure steps into faith. It was called Castle Rock, near Sydenham Durban. On the bedroom floor of the mostly unfurnished apartment, was a strange heap. It was piled high with shirts and dresses, jeans and shoes and dozens of other items of clothing that were part of my life. I was in a frenzy. I wanted to walk the path with just two dresses and a pair of Green Cross sandals. I wanted to not have to waste another second deciding on my outfit for the day. The vanity of grooming and trying to be attractive were a waste of more precious time; having to coordinate, match, be in style, be current, be pleasing to society, engaging, ever engaging in frivolity and so I asked my mum to come and receive the odd pile of leftovers from her daughter who was changing not just her faith but her wardrobe too.

The night my mother arrived with my brother Eugene and his wife Lulu was a night that must be described in detail. They knocked on the door. Eugene already had his video camera going to document what his sister had been up to in all the months she'd been so absent from her family.

It was then that the hilarious, incongruous state of our living and how it would seem to others, became apparent. The red light on his camera pointed to the curtain on the patio door. It was made up entirely of A4 sheets of paper covered in Qurannic verses that had been taped together by Isa. The lounge, if you could call it that, was bare, save for a brown and black portrait of the Ka'ba on the one wall. Eugene couldn't contain his laughter at the emptiness and austerity of it all and it was just what was needed to break the glaciers of cold scepticism that my mother and sister-in-law were trying to suppress. We all laughed as I tried to explain why we were choosing to live with as little belongings as possible. It seemed that the more I explained the louder we laughed. You sleep where? On the floor? You do what? Take in complete strangers and beggars off the street? You pray how often? Five times a day? More? Laughter was the medicine that helped us find each other again that night.

As they prepared to leave, my mum with the armfuls of clothing I had abandoned, and my brother, with a fresh, if not clearer, understanding of what we were doing, I felt that I was home again and not so alone anymore.

The memory makes me smile as the last tufts of evicted hair cosy up to its partners in the packet. I felt free. I wondered what my husband would say as he had no idea what I was up to in that bedroom.

I called out to him and he left the heated discussion about religion and life taking place on the floor in the adjoining room with our religious teacher. As the door opened, the expression on his face went from an enquiring one to one registering complete shock. His wife, who just earlier had a crown of curly locks, looked like a Buddhist nun.

I called the imam's wife into the room and she too was stunned. 'But why, Iman?' That seemed to be a question that stalked me a lot in the beginning. As I explained, they understood but still felt I was taking things too far.

15

Chadors, Clerics and Change

As our flight to Iran prepared for landing at Tehran's Mehrabad Airport, I wondered what Ayatollah Ruhollah Khomeini must have been thinking the day he left Paris after more than fourteen years in nomadic exile. He was coming home. Finally. Preparing to be lifted high on the shoulders of revolutionary celebration on the 1st of February 1979.

That day, millions of Iranians turned out to welcome him home. The streets outside the airport heaved with delirium as Iranians came from far and wide to drink in the euphoria of change. The Shah, a man loathed for opulent living and a brutal crackdown on dissent through a vicious secret police called the Savak, had been overthrown. A new order was about to take over. A time of decadence and the state's lapdog deference to the West was roughly ended. The families of means that disagreed with the change, or those who feared reprisals had fled, leaving behind Samovar sets and carpets, extended family and generations of history.

I had heard their stories at Persian restaurants in South Africa and carpet shops in the US. They would lament over the state of politics in their country, questioning the religious hegemony, bitter about why they had to flee. They still seemed wounded. When they shared their memories of home, it was with an eye that seemed to see, in real time, what they were describing. A place where the pomegranates were bursting with juicy rubies, the water tasted like angels' tears, soft and sweet, the orchards were more lush, the spring more resplendent than anywhere else in the world and their art and poetry, divinely inspired. Their exile had the opposite effect of sharpening their memory.

As Khomeini no doubt looked down during his landing he may have caught a glimpse of the waves of people thronging the Azadi (freedom or liberty) Tower. He was asked, so the story goes, by foreign journalists how he was feeling. It seems he kept his thoughts closely guarded. I'd read in John Simpson's *Lifting the Veil: Life in Revolutionary Iran* that he answered with one word. *Hitchi.* A word that means 'nothing' in Persian.

I found it hard to imagine that he was not affected by a significant moment in history for whom so many had suffered and sacrificed. A vision was set, fixed and scaffolded by a twin desire to purge the country of excess and its distracting influences and also to resist any attempt by Western countries to undermine the new order. And while Khomeini recognised women as being a key part of their struggle, at the forefront of protests, he also exhorted them to take up the chador as a symbol of the revolution. And it seemed to me when I was there that wearing it still communicated that message very strongly.

It's even more significant than the stories I've read recently of women emboldened to discard their hijab and begin to dangerously defy the religious laws (this seemed impossible when I lived there). The voices of the youth craving change and freedom were but whispers I heard floating along the corridors at work but now they are rising steadily; critical and outspoken. The Iran of today is in a very different place, with a lot of contemporary issues to face and address in a time where the authority of the religious class is being questioned and challenged in ever braver and more outspoken ways.

But this was Iman, version 1997, a believer who thirstily lapped up the victory of religion over secularism and opulence. I had stars in my eyes as we landed that day in Iran. The trauma of our South African goodbye was replaced by the euphoria of finally being here, in this place, Khomeini's Iran.

We landed. I was in awe. Iran is unlike anything I'd ever seen before. Every woman was covered up. Eyes don't meet. The smell of Iranian food, which I would become totally addicted to, greets my nose, unfamiliar and strange. The animated and melodic sounds of Farsi being spoken confuses me; I have barely learnt to speak it. We make it through passport control and are then outside on the pavement, watching people manage their bags, children and dangerously busy traffic.

Our teacher is waiting. Sayed Hosseini has a huge smile on his face. He has missed us and he's excited to show us his country. There is a small car waiting to make the drive to the holy city of Qom, an hour's drive away. It is there that separate universities for men and women are. It is there that our son will be born. It is there that we will take our first real steps towards throwing ourselves into the holy book. But it is also there, as I found out later, that the seeds of my disquiet would slowly travel on a zephyr and take gentle root in my garden of consciousness.

As much as I try to focus on and feel everything, it is the rising nausea from inside my core that dominates. I'm in the early stages of pregnancy. Fever and headaches assault me relentlessly and I cannot keep anything down. All I think about as I lie on the back seat of the car, looking for comfort in the moon, is that I want to stop moving, find a cool compress for my throbbing head and a way to steady my stomach.

We arrive in Qom. It is late. We pull up outside a double-storeyed guest house. The pungent aroma of what would later turn out to be my favourite Iranian dish, hits me and I strain to climb the stairs. I wave away the welcoming gestures of the slightly bowing, smiling housekeeper and signal for the bathroom. My shoes are violently kicked off at the door and before they are even concussed against the adjoining wall, I am already hugging the basin ejecting a large volume of nothing.

There is nothing worse, surely, than having the overwhelming urge to throw up when there is nothing to displace. Instead, your insides convulse like a centrifuge and the grip on your throat feels tight, like wearing a corset three sizes too small. Finally, the urge passes, my watering eyes are wiped and I can now take in my surroundings. Ah, the toilet is a long drop. Plus, a hose; nice for the ease of washing 'down below'.

I return to the vast but cold lounge. A gas heater is fired up to counter the chill and I pad across an intricately designed carpet. There, in the centre of the rug, a clear sheet of plastic is spread. On it are steaming bowls of a greenish-brown stew, veined with thin tributaries of oil. I can see chunks of red meat, red beans and a bobbing ballet of fat, brown limes. The green is due to several types of leafy vegetables that have been cooked down.

On the side of the 'Ghormah sabzi' (the green stuff's Farsi name) is a mountain of white rice, liberally decorated with streaks of gloriously reddish, yellow saffron and bright green slivers of pistachio. Red beads of sweet and sour 'zereshk' (a type of dried grape) dot the surface. It looks like something out of an ancient cookery book. Shot glasses of tea are flamboyantly poured from a large and long-spouted pot. Their scalding contents make it difficult to hold and drink, let alone expertly siphon though a sugar cube placed in the front of your mouth between one's top and bottom teeth.

Iranians in many parts of the country tend to eat on the floor and it took weeks of pins and needles for me to perfect my sitting posture.

But the sight of food and its intense taste send me right back to the bathroom. This was to become a pattern in the months ahead of what early on promised to be a difficult pregnancy. I got thinner and thinner and terribly sick.

We settled in for the night, grabbing two home-made mattresses (really just a stitching together of several blankets). I lay down and sleep came quickly. The next morning, slightly disorientated, I began to remember where we were. I opened the tap, thirsty for a drink of cold water. As the liquid hit my tongue, I sensed something was wrong. It tasted strange.

Then I remembered Sayed telling us that this was the famous but unpalatable taste of Qom water, 'Aab-e shoor', subtly infected by prolific salt pans near the town.

Later we'd queue with plastic canisters and wait for the mobile tankers that brought fresh water twice a week. It was tedious and made buying bottled water far more appealing. I would discover, much to my shock and surprise, in a country that exports oil, petrol was cheaper than water.

After two days in the holy city, spent mostly drinking tea at Sayed's house, served by a meticulous host, his wife Mastana, we were back in the car and heading on our first road trip. We sped towards Tehran and beyond, along the Persian Gulf Highway that snaked through the ribs of the Alborz Mountains. I couldn't stop pointing at things and sighing. It was like seeing a mobile, dynamic canvas that presented something unique and gasp-inducing every minute.

After a few hours of driving we stopped in the exquisite coastal city of Chalus. I imprudently sit on the cold beach, which is the colour of crushed coal, trying to preserve every emotion and experience in my diary, while the melancholic romance of small waves escaping the vast bosom of the Caspian Sea, kissed my toes before being pulled away again.

We get in a cable car that pulls us up the mountain until we reach what I would only describe as Eden's sister. The Namak Abrud Forest Park takes your breath away with its towering green showstoppers of a variety of trees, including ash, that have been there for centuries. I muse as to what these trees must have seen in the town below as conquering armies and rebels rolled through at various points in history, desperate and determined to take ownership of new territories. But for now the only conquering being done is by the mist as it starts to roll in, taking over and overwhelming the trees and rocks.

A hot cup of tea is placed in my hand. As I carefully sip its fragrantly warm contents, I also drink in the beauty and mystique of a beautifully preserved corner of the world.

The next day it's back in the car and on towards Mashad, Iran's second largest city. It's there where I would horrify my hosts with my insatiable penchant for drinking milk boiled with turmeric powder and ginger. 'Iman, your baby will turn out yellow,' they warned.

Then it's onto a wedding party and a visit to what I'm told is the largest mosque in the world, bearing the holy shrine of Imam Reza, the eighth Imam of Shia Islam.

It was a culture shock staying with our teacher's relatives. Sleeping on the floor, eating on the floor, being introduced to an entirely new range of food and speaking hesitantly to people who'd never had a conversation in English before. It is significant to note that when you believe in something, all discomfort floats away like feathers on a breeze. You're prepared, even welcoming of unusual or uncomfortable things, and every fresh experience is exciting.

The kindness of people stuck out the most for me. Everywhere we went there was only a welcome embrace, curious questions and generosity.

A week after our outing we were back in Qom, ready to settle down and prepare for our studies at the university. Our flat was on a main street noisily grumbling with heavy trucks and taxis. It was small and crowded by a giant poster of Khomeini and a desk stuffed with Qurans, Islamic philosophy and law books. And all day long, as became customary, a pot of tea infused with cardamom pods and cinnamon, brewed on the stove. We were ready, cup of tea in hand for anyone who might stop by unannounced.

We began to meet students from all over the world who flocked to Iran for religious instruction. Nights were filled with debate and days were for university. Soon we fell into a routine. Thursdays were reserved for buying a small box of pretty, delicate cakes expertly made by a corner bakery, which we'd share over tea with friends after the communal Friday prayer called Jumma. This was the official start to the weekend.

Later in the summer, when the sun beat down and it was 45 degrees in the shade, the only sensible time to go outside was after the Asr (afternoon) prayer. We'd emerge from our apartment and walk to a nearby park or to shops which stayed open past midnight in the open market. We discovered a delicious banana milkshake called 'sheer moz' which was freshly blitzed by food vendors in carts on every street corner. Carrying that in one hand and a packet of 'togmeh', a mix of nuts and seeds, in the other, we'd stroll contentedly, eating and drinking and watching families picnicking under the moon.

Occasionally we would get into a taxi and head for Tehran. There we would catch a bus or taxi to the cableway and have a picnic in the sprawl of the Alborz Mountains that towered over the massive city. In the winter, young men and daring women would snowboard on the powdered slopes.

Sometimes we'd stroll through the popular park, Park-e-Mellat, which was at the top of the longest street in Iran. The famed Valiasr Street was lined with tall plane trees which watched themselves bald as their leaves lost their grip in autumn and floated into gutters channelling rapidly running water. Shopping malls, really fancy ones, are dotted on either side of the road and it had the same cosmopolitan feel of a major city anywhere in the world.

The difference was the music of the Persian language, the buttoned-up coats and scarves worn by all the women and that fact that the burger shops would not only sell you a patty and fries, but you could also have the option of sheep's brain.

In the park though, something curious stood out. Groups

of young men and women walked past each other, clearly interested in one another judging by the quick, flirty looks they flashed, a barely audible question of a name thrown into the space between them, and the light giggle or smile that was given in response. But there was an unspoken, invisible barrier between them. Religious convention. A convention that was enforced and vigilantly monitored by the groups of religious police, or Brown Shirts, as they were known to us.

There seemed to be no room for young people to get to know each other in the way that was considered normal back home. These monitors admonished girls about their exposed hair, instructing them to cover up and warned boys off getting too close to them. I saw the boys' opposition in their frustrated faces and sullen looks. It seemed strange and bizarre to me and I didn't like it. But I accepted it as part of the social hygiene promoted by the faith expressed in that country.

We'd return to Qom after these visits feeling tired. Months later, I'd managed to learn to read and write Persian fairly well because the language instructor would not take questions in English or any other language for that matter. I felt like a kid at nursery school in the beginning when we were taught really basic lessons, like what an ambulance or a car was, and then having to repeat the words like children, 'aaam-boo-lahns' (ambulance) or 'mah-sheen' (car).

As we neared the one-year mark, I realised that I did not

want to study religious law. There were many reasons for this, chief among which was the realisation that I had serious issues about my prospects of becoming a female Islamic jurist. It was a happy coincidence then that because I'd already done some freelance work for the national broadcaster they asked me to be the face of a new TV current affairs programme. Recorded in English it hosted a variety of political commentators, visiting dignitaries and religious commentators. It gave me a greater understanding of the geo-political juggling that President Mohammad Khatami had to perform in trying to manage Iran's new policy of detente with a world formally closed off.

We packed, took our son Muhammad, who was now a few months old, and headed for Tehran.

16

The Night I Almost Killed the Party in Iran

The morning of our arrival in another of Iran's holy cities, Mashad, brought with it an invitation to a wedding. Our teacher's wife, Fatima, had readied the house for the celebration of a friend's daughter's union to a boy from the community. Each of the two floors of the house were dedicated to the festivities that would be enjoyed separately by the men and the women.

Our hosts were keen to show me off as the 'girl from Africa' to guests who rarely had the opportunity to interact with foreigners. Over a breakfast of 'barbari' (a delicious bread sprinkled with sesame seeds, made minutes before by the naan vahi on the street corner), cherry jam, butter, nuts and yoghurt, washed down with shot glasses of strong black Ahmad orange blossom tea, we talked about Iranian tradition and weddings. While at the same time they tried to overlook my disgusting practice of adding milk to 'a perfectly, perfect cup of cardamom-infused tea'!

The kids (who were fairly proficient in English) translated for their mum and soon I learnt that a wedding in Iran brought with it the similar stresses of a wedding anywhere else in the world. There were the flashpoints for disagreements and anxiety from family rivalries over the guest list, the menu, the costs and most importantly the dowry. In many societies a dowry is still an expression of prestige and value that conveys to the community how much you and your family are worth. If the groom's family doesn't offer an appropriate amount it's seen as an insult. I laughed when I thought about my own dowry; one old silver motorbike, sold for our rent deposit a few days after receiving it!

That day was a blur of calls to prayer, then lunch and then tea and soon it was time for me to experience my first real social gathering in Iran. The girls and their mum went to get changed and made up. I stayed in my room, unsure of what to expect and not feeling well enough to muster a smile and make conversation. My body was still having an argument with my pregnancy hormones as waves of nausea washed over it. I had taken to eating tuna fish and vinegar, trying in vain to find viciously hot chillies to accompany it and steady the rolling ship that was permanently the state of my tummy. I was missing home and the inability to indulge in my pregnant craving for Niknaks and sour cream, biltong and gherkins was leading to an irritating crying-for-no-reason syndrome.

My nausea was worsened by a newly developed aversion to a particular brand of shampoo and soap which, to this day, has the power to take me right back to our life in Iran. Fatima and the girls found me back in the reception room and seemed surprised that I was wearing almost exactly what I had had on earlier that day but they barely had time to say anything to me before the first guests started to arrive.

One by one women shimmied into the room, in full party mode. I was surprised. I don't know why I thought Iran would be a place of prayer-filled austerity and black veils.

Well, there were the black veils, especially in the sacred city of Mashad where some of Shia Islam's holiest shrines were but these were exclusively for outdoor wear. If you had guests and were indoors you would wear a softer version of the forbidding chador, one probably adorned with flowers and light colours. And in the capital Tehran, as I would later see, many women favoured the stylish coat, called a roupush, available in many colours with headscarves to match. Fashion seemed important there and the flash of the coveted blonde hair was not an uncommon sight.

As the wedding guests swept into the room on the crest of laughter and chatter, I stayed put in my little corner, cross-legged on the plush, red carpet. I wore one of my two outfits, if you could even call them that, the plain, black cotton dress with a plain, black scarf.

The women were speaking in Persian and their faces told me they were asking our host about the girl in the corner.

'Emrooz ahmad, az Afrika joonoob hast,' (She just came today, she is from South Africa) Fatima said smilingly, as if I was some exciting package that had been hand-delivered that morning.

The women crowded around me. They were eager to hear stories from South Africa but looked puzzled. 'You look more Iraqi, than African. You could even be Afghan or from Pakistan!' they exclaimed. I laughed. We talked about how Africans can have mixed ancestry, how in some cases we carry the violence of colonialism in our genes through forced marriages and rape or, in other cases, falling in love and creating mixed-race children. And how we look different region to region.

And as they let down their guard, and I mine, we all relaxed. I was amazed, perhaps shocked is a better word, to see how well put together they were. I was expecting to see not only a country of minarets and national symbols and the occasional building draped in 'Death to America, Death to Israel' slogans but of people who shunned frivolity. I was quickly being shown otherwise.

As a Western girl, I knew good fashion when I saw it. The very best dresses, suits and silky slacks from Europe clung to their trim bodies. Gucci? Gaultier? Hermès? Seriously? In Iran's holy city of Mashad? I could feel the imams' disapproving stroking of beards and shaking of heads.

Their hairstyles were a sight to behold as imaginary harps and violins accompanied the fall of the veil with the revelation of glorious bouffant blonde updos and glittering jewellery. The extravagant blouses and pants, or suffocation-inducing tight skirts and dresses, were gaily paraded as laughter rose and mingled with abundant compliments. *'Ghely ghoskel Khanom!'* (Very beautiful lady!)

They were just like women everywhere, I thought. Look good, feel good, have a good time, no matter what you believe or where you live.

As they spoke, they arched beautiful, lush eyebrows with just the exact brow bone to hair ratio. As an aside: you do not mess with Iranian women and their eyebrows. It's a thing. It's a serious thing. I would conjecture that next to carpets, pistachio nuts and oil, immaculately landscaped eyebrows are a national asset. They have it down to a fine art.

Months later when I hosted a current affairs show for the public broadcaster my make-up artist would sigh and threaten to throw her tweezers at me. I had plucked, no, evicted, my eyebrows so violently that all that was left was a severe suggestion of hair that resembled the thin border lines on a map. She spent months nursing the fullness back into existence while creating the illusion of perfection with well-placed strokes of powder and pencil. *'Chera arbrew shoma ghordeed khanom?'* (Why did you eat your eyebrows, lady?) she would tut-tut and then assure me she would fix it all.

But back to the wedding. I think I disappointed the women in that bland dress of mine. I think they must have been expecting more from a foreigner. Something more exotic. But they were so kind and so interested in my story. Fatima explained that I was a journalist who had abandoned her career to study Islamic law at the famed Jami'at al-Zahra in Qom, a Vatican-like city. She told them that I had recently converted to Islam. This statement appeared to draw the most interest. They wanted to know why. I explained the months on the pier, the endless reading and searching and the intoxicating tug I felt at the sound of the Quran being recited.

They were hooked.

We could hear the laughter of the men sneaking up the stairs from the floor below but all ears were trained on the words tumbling from my mouth. As I spoke, Fatima's daughter

Sumeya translated. She laughed uproariously at my terrible Persian as I tried here and there to make the conversation flow more smoothly. I could only muster the most basic of sentences with an accent so bad Hafiz would wail in his grave out of pity for the language!

But then feeling so comfortable, I did the unexpected.

I uncovered my head. As I placed the scarf on my lap, a collective gasp sucked the life out of the air. The sight of my almost bald head jolted the women before they even had the opportunity to lower their eyebrows that shot up to show restrained politeness. A woman's hair is her crown and across the Muslim world there is a practice of reserving its splendour for your husband and those you can't marry. Hair is a potent manifestation of beauty and yet here was this strange woman sitting without any. Why? That familiar question.

I began to share my unorthodox views on beauty and worship and I revealed my pursuit of the death of self and vanity to focus solely on God and godly things (it all sounds so alien to my ears now). They were quiet but drew closer. It wasn't long before tears begin to fall, not just from my eyes but from theirs too. I cry because a crowd of images flood to my mind, of a world in which all supplicate, all surrender personal desire for collective benefit. A potent montage flashes before my eyes, hidden from view, of those who fought against injustice in the name of Islam and died for it.

THE NIGHT I ALMOST KILLED THE PARTY IN IRAN

In my mind I think of the Prophet, his family, their martyrdom at Karbala at the hands of an evil ruler and of empty-saddled horses returning to camp with arrows in their sides, bearing news of the massacre of their riders. More tears flow.

The women say they understand. In that moment I recall feeling like they felt indicted. Here was a convert who reminded them that proximity to God is distance from vanity. Years later as I remember this moment I am still emotional. But for different reasons. I felt at the time a supreme connection to an expression of faith, of Iman, in this way. It almost feels alien now as if I am talking about another person and I suppose I am. I am light years away from this version of myself.

The women gather my hands, kneel next to me and pray, a dua is sombrely offered, a string of prayer beads is rubbed and shaken and as we wipe away the tears and smile at each other, I encourage a return to the festivities. Reluctantly, but gradually, that pretty, unique style of Iranian dance, with twirling wrists, shaking hips and expressive eyes gets underway and the only victim in the scene – the handmade carpet – becomes more than the catcher of tears, more than a mantelpiece for abandoned scarves but an altar for rhythmic feet and a table for a feast.

17

Navigating the Slipstream

The Islamic Republic of Iran Broadcasting Authority (IRIB) was an impressively sprawling modern facility situated in Northern Tehran. Before my husband and I received our permanent access tags, we would have to go through the tedious ritual of saying our unfamiliar names to long-suffering staff who had to deal with foreigners from all over the world. I'd have to really enunciate, 'Va-neh-sah. Raa-pee-tee.' I'd chuckle to myself and it would take a few more times before the guards eventually let me through. We'd walk towards the foreign hub, which broadcast programmes on both television and radio, in many languages, to many parts of the world.

We hosted a radio show that received postcards (remember them?) from listeners around the world, especially the Indian subcontinent. It was exciting hearing from people sharing the stories of their lives in their part of the world. This was long before social media networks closed almost all the gaps in communication and it was a quaint and intimate way to connect with people.

At the end of the month we'd get paid in US dollars, which made the conversion at the bank an amusing exercise. We would each have to carry a backpack to hold the cash after withdrawing our salary in local currency. Iranians are not shy to ask how much you earn and this was made clear to me one day while waiting for a bus with a crowd of people gathered tightly together. A woman we worked with in the English division at the broadcaster, who spoke no English, turned to me and asked rather loudly, *'Maheey, che khat megeery?* (How much do you earn monthly?). Everyone turned around, not even pretending to be disinterested, and waited to hear my answer. I told the woman that in my culture it was impolite to ask such a personal question and she raised an eyebrow at me and looked away, leaving me to manage the awkward gulf of silence that grew in the space between us.

One of the crew at the IRIB was a striking man; tall and beautiful with lips that elegantly curled around each word he said. Let's call him Reza. I knew instinctively what he was trying to hide; I had always had gay men as friends, from my hairdresser to a wider friendship circle before converting to Islam. So I was deeply affected when I realised that living in Islam, and in Iran, meant that the LGBTQIA community could never be 'out'. I had not even considered the consequence the laws of religion would have on homosexuals and it was just dawning on me that he could never be himself. He could never go out and find love like other people. He was forever banished to the shadows within himself, cunningly navigating the slipstream between the truth of who he really was and the reality that the truth could never be naked in the light.

His was an uncertain existence behind drawn curtains, anxiety and conflicted piety because he had grown up in a world taught to revile the creature he was. He seemed racked by guilt and shame in a society whose oxygen is faith and yet he would defend his Islam. I did not probe too much. And since I was dressed in the chador, which was at that time really a symbol of not just fitting into Iranian society but of supporting the religious order, I had to earn his trust in letting me see him in a more honest way than he would let others see him. Reza toned down his fire in a place where the 'abomination' that was him, could be severely punished and he was left with little hope of actually finding true love one day or of ever being able to show affection in public.

There was a lot for me to take in, in Iran. I had to be

open to learning new things and questioning my own frame of living in the romance of a post-revolutionary society. I learnt that the price of war was high and that many people lived with the consequences of nerve damage many years after the eight-year war with Iraq. And that if people weren't physically scarred then they were emotionally and mentally so. I found a rich and deep philosophical and art culture that located a deadly history in a way that brought hope and beauty. And I loved the humour of the shop owners who would tell you there was 'no charge' for something you wanted to buy, when in fact you still had to pay.

Iran was also once home to the largest refugee population in the world and became the waiting room for the suspended dreams of people escaping war. People like the Kuwaitis, the Iraqis but mostly Afghans.

Often one would see, in the glow of a lamp in half-finished high-rise buildings that were beginning to spring up rapidly in Iran, the shadows of men who seemed to be in limbo. They were there to work, separated from their families and in many instances only able to go home once a year. Many of them were the muscle and sinew and sweat of the burgeoning construction industry as apartment blocks began to reach for the sky in the plush northern parts of Tehran.

One day while walking on the street I stopped to talk to an elderly Afghani man, curious about what he was doing and where his family was. He told me in Pashto, which I could just about understand, that his body was aching, that he'd fled the instability and war in Afghanistan and that he worked in Iran to send money to his family that couldn't flee with him. He also said he felt like a second-class citizen where his labour was good enough for Iranian society but he wasn't. I encountered this story a few times and not just with Afghans but even with fellow South Africans who would hear the word, 'nesfeshab', being thrown around when they walked by. 'Nesfeshab' means 'midnight' and they regularly felt the sulphur of xenophobia in a place where seeing Africans was still strange.

Iranian marriage, in my own experience, is a delicate, negotiated process in which there is much more at stake than just whether two people can puzzle-fit and live a life of happiness. It is about status, class, family name, honour and prestige. The whole vetting system sounded so exhausting and I worked with many women who said they would never get married because either the man's family was not wealthy, or he wasn't as educated as she was, or because her family didn't think their union would enhance their social prospects. Young women would confide in me about being set up with a man much older than them because he was rich, or about how unemployment had made many available men unviable.

Then there was also the discreet 'shopping around' by a

man for a second wife. I became friends with a woman who was happy to cook special dishes like 'Morgh Polow' (chicken and rice), and 'Sholezard' (a saffron pudding) for her husband who would visit weekly from Tabriz. She would work herself into a frenzy making sure her eyebrows were plucked, her skin looked youthful and her figure was tight. Her husband was a businessman who already had a wife but 'needed' the variety (apparently) of a woman who had lived in America. She wavered, like many women I met, between peace with the situation and anxiety about whether she'd be cut loose or whether he would take a younger bride.

On the rare occasion when we happened to visit and her husband was there, I got the distinct sense that he thought he was superior to her and that she was lucky to have someone like him. They were together because of a provision for temporary marriage. A union that can last anywhere between an hour and 99 years and that's sealed with a mutual agreement on dowry. I didn't like the sound of it and it was something not really talked about in conservative circles.

But this type of marriage, 'mu'tah', was a reality. After work at the IRIB we sometimes went onto the main street to buy dinner. A short distance from the entrance was, what I later learnt, a known spot for picking up women. I saw beautiful women, heavily made-up, a flash of blonde hair and a glimpse of their neckline, quickly get into cars that seemed in a hurry to move along. I naively thought that that sort of thing could never happen in the Islamic Republic with its morality police and fear of authority.

I knew a teacher of religion who I'd respected, confess to having had several mu'tahs. Years later when we saw him long after we left Iran, I learnt that his latest arrangement was with a woman much younger than his three other wives and the story shared many parallels with what we call the 'Blesser' culture in South Africa. An older man of means having at his disposal a young woman (or women) dependent on those means and having to 'pay' with her charms.

Later, I heard terrible stories of how women were treated badly, verbally abused and were powerless to do anything because while legally sanctioned it was still a big taboo in Iran. It's fed into the sanctioned single-use discard culture, which seemed to be growing if I believed the stories I heard. I myself had the briefest of brushes with this one night, many years later, while waiting on the street for a taxi.

I'd gone back to Iran do a story about the nuclear saga and to hear from politicians their version about whether the country was developing nukes. I had the night off and was standing on the road with a young woman, the daughter of a close friend. I signalled randomly for a taxi and a silver Peugeot pulled up. Something about the grey-haired man seemed different, maybe it was the slightest flash of excitement in his eyes, but I didn't really compute and started to get into the car when my friend pulled me sharply back. The driver looked at me and smiled as I quickly withdrew. My friend said to me, 'Iman, that's not a taxi it's a man looking for sigheh or mu'tah.' I asked how she knew and she just nodded her head and said she just knew. I laughed, slightly shocked but also slightly relieved. Things had changed; things were more 'out' than since the last time I'd been in Iran.

18

Clingwrap Sex

We once lived in a basic subsidised housing block near the famous Oriental Plaza in Fordsburg in Johannesburg. It marked our first reunion with the city that provided a waiting room ahead of our journey years earlier to Iran. This time was palpably different. The stars of new discovery were less bright than when we'd left. We were also a family, with two small children and a constellation of problems to manage.

    A biryani of people lived in the block. Young, corporate types, married couples with small children, some elderly people on the ground floor and overtly religious folk like us with the flowing robes of orthodox Islam. Our big, white, but old Mercedes Benz parked in the communal bays next to racier, fancier counterparts whose owners I thought could surely afford better quarters. But no matter, here we all were greeting each other on weekends while children played and cars were washed.

I would shuffle up the two flights of stairs to our tiny flat, gathering the folds of the voluminous, black chador I insisted on wearing from time to time, a familiar, exotic scent carrying me up each step. My senses were transported by the smell of the most delicious curries to places where elephants carried people and stories were told under a banyan tree. I imagined the steaming pots gurgling at the ritual assembly of recipes passed down via jealously guarded secrets shared only between mother and daughter, aunty and niece.

Without fail, as I neared the door behind which culinary magic was being made, I would hear it close abruptly, in the style typical of someone who is peeping or eavesdropping. I was intrigued. I wanted to find out who the mysterious curry alchemist was and why she was too shy to say hello.

My opportunity came one day when I needed some dhania to finish off a dish and in desperation I turned to the mysterious door slammer, who I knew would be home. I knocked. Nothing. I knocked again, several times, but still nothing. Just as I rolled my eyes in frustration and prepared to walk away, I heard a click and a nose poked out from behind the door.

'Salaam,' it said.

'Wasalaam,' I answered, relieved. 'How are you? My sister, do you have some dhania to spare? My curry's almost done and I've run out. I was going to ask Majida downstairs but she is so judgemental, she would think me a most inadequate wife if I dared reveal I'd run out!'

I began to giggle, totally unsure of what to expect but surprised at what happened next. A responding giggle rippled across the threshold and soon the door was opened wide enough for me to see the woman's face and finally define the person at the top of the stairs as more than just the 'hijabi peeper'. She invited me in and before long our relationship blossomed into a tree bigger than just a handful of aromatic curry leaves.

Months later, masala chai and jalebis were routinely exchanged over conversations that brought down both our headscarves and our guard.

I heard about her family, also from Durban, who had arranged her marriage to a boy of their choosing. A boy she met mere weeks before the wedding and with whom she had no previous frame of reference. But their families matched, their backgrounds matched and most importantly their religion matched. Islam was culture, was life, was everything.

And so it was that everyone gathered as the imam solemnised their bond and they were sent into the world as man and wife. Not long after, two cherubs came along and their joy should have been sealed and complete.

Zaytoon, I shall call her, made many confessions to me in those snatched hours between prayers, cooking, my working and looking after my own children and she dealing with hers. Most of those confessions, the most profound ones, were about her husband, Ismail. She had learnt, quite by chance, that Ismail had shacked up with another woman some months earlier. She now found herself in a polygamous marriage with a woman she did not know and hadn't met, let alone a woman she'd been asked to approve. This was the first inner silencing that came from being left out of such a life-altering decision by a man whose affections were proving to be questionable.

More months of conversations and roti-rolling competitions (mine still came out skew) followed before Zaytoon had something else to say about her husband. We sat down on the second-hand blue, floral sofa. She stared out of the window, beyond the balcony overlooking taxis speeding down noisy Bree Street. I watched her hesitation give way to a flood of words that boasted in those moments her mastery of being able to speak without needing to breathe.

She reminded me of an excursion we had taken with another Muslim sister of ours some weeks prior.

As with many women whose husbands' affections are doubted or dubious, or which have to be competed for and shared, or imprisoned and guaranteed, you drive yourself crazy with the belief that somehow if you looked better, opened your legs wider and more often, spoke less, thought less and were simply less, you could secure his love and loyalty. (Isn't that warped?)

So it was that Zaytoon and I landed up in a Lola Montez shop in Randburg for the very first time. You can imagine the scene. Two Muslim women at a private, high-end sex shop looking for the accoutrements of pleasure and attention-seeking and holding. The one staff member, a gracious and non-judgemental lady, was bemused that women like us had blood that could burn so red and so hot. She was learning that actually women behind the veil were not anatomically, emotionally, or intellectually different to sisters anywhere in the world. They were also women who could be racy and passionate, women who actually had sex and wanted to enjoy it. Her body language communicated the education that was happening in the store that day. An education that challenged the otherisation that stalks groups of people you don't know too much about but who you make grand assumptions about.

Anyway, I stroked feather dusters and furry handcuffs, laughing and slightly embarrassed that we had actually carried out our dare to come and see how to spice things up in our marriages. I settled on a bustier and a short whip. Zaytoon nervously grabbed red fishnets, a satin teddy and a short, red baby-doll gown complete with downy, feathery trimmings.

We left the shop feeling a little sinful but rationalised that it was for our husbands and by extension for the Deen, the faith, so it was okay. We each nervously went home and by now early evening had begun to dim the lights in the sky. It is at this point that Zaytoon picks up her story.

When she got home, Ismail was working at the small, cheap dining-room table in the centre of their one-bedroom flat. In the bedroom their two children were fast asleep and definitely being serenaded by angels. The helper had left. This was Zaytoon's chance! She greeted her husband but all she got in return was his back and a low grunt. Whatever he was doing was absorbing his attention.

Perfect. She stole into the bathroom and took a light wash of the most important strategic places and wiggled herself into the slutty trappings of our afternoon shopping. The final touch was a pair of stilettos bought on a Truworths account and she was ready to make her grand, if unusual, entrance. Not feeling entirely brave, she told me, she drew over the lingerie a neat, housewifey gown, to heighten the surprise.

Zaytoon slid onto a sofa in eyeshot of the table. She sat in a way that was unusual for her; she was leaning back, suggestively. She told me it probably looked comical but she stayed put. Still nothing from Ismail. She let the gown slip, her confidence almost did too but she pressed on and cleared her throat.

At last, Ismail looked over and took in what would have been a shocking scene. His usually vanilla wife was sitting in the uniform of a stripper, perched seductively on the couch, clearly thinking about sex.

What he could not see was the silent movie that was rolling just behind Zaytoon's eyelids. It was a horror story, really, of betrayal through the many women she knew he'd slept with and the 'secret' marriage he continued to deny.

It was excruciating for me to think how she could even contemplate having this man around her, let alone on her skin or inside her body.

But her resoluteness intersected with the triumph of his nafs (desire), and she told me she was emboldened to approach him. All this was new and scary to her, describing how vulnerable she felt and how fragile and shattered she would have been if his answer was rejection.

They kissed. Awkwardly. So much was standing between their lips. She took his hand and led him to the spare bed crouching in the corner of the room. There she attempted to do all the things she thought he would like; touching him, letting her mouth anoint every inch of his body. He responded as men do, greedily and selfishly. And then, without asking what she'd like, or whether she was ready for entry, he prepared to bring matters to a head and a close and readied himself for penetration. But she stopped him.

Zaytoon looked even more lost as she was talking to me. I'm sure her eyes no longer registered the tree outside nor the sunlight that was streaming into the room. It was like she was reliving every agonising moment. My heart was suspended.

She said, 'I looked up at him and I began to feel hot and humiliated from having to ask him to go down. I couldn't believe I was actually asking him. I had to bully the words up my throat because I couldn't believe I had to ask for something he should have cared enough to offer, to make sure, to make me happy.'

I was reviled by every single word. I also felt awkward but was so conscious of how much she needed me in those moments.

She continued, 'Ismail paused for a second, looked at me like I was stupid and said, "I don't like it."'

But, she continued, she somehow found the courage to activate her voice and in an almost strangulated way, whispered her insistence. 'Please.'

And then the unthinkable happened.

Ismail rolled off the bed. He walked, penis still erect but slapping his thighs, towards the kitchen. Zaytoon heard shuffling and the annoyed opening and closing of drawers.

'What are you doing?' she asked worriedly, as she lay there in the room growing colder with every second.

Finally, it seemed he had found what he had been looking for and he returned. His tall frame dwarfed the bed. Zaytoon looked up, confused. Then he said, 'Open.'

With a flourish, Ismail tore something and she heard the familiar plasticky crackle of clingwrap. The same clingwrap roll she covered last night's chicken pies with, the same clingwrap roll she wrapped his lunch with that morning, was now the same clingwrap he was covering her parting with.

She was shocked. 'What's happening?' she cried out but she was silenced. Again. Silenced by her sense of worthlessness, of not being entitled to enjoyment or reciprocity. Silenced by the insinuation that she was dirty and disgusting.

All she heard, alongside the roar of her shame, were the determined, marine-like sounds of saliva and the scratchy bristles of a young beard amplifying into a crescendo in her ears. It was awful. He was going down on her using the plastic as a barrier. He didn't want to actually taste her, he wanted nothing to do with even her scent.

Tears began to roll down her cheeks. I wanted to reach out to her and hold her hand or grab her shoulders but I sensed this would halt the crucial and necessary unbundling of her soul that was happening before my eyes.

She described even more detail and the images screeched

into my imagination. She lay there paralysed. Parts of her were disintegrating like an effervescent tablet in a glass of water. She was being fragmented. Every reluctant slurp and readjustment of plastic sloughed off another piece of her. It was akin to dying. Ismail didn't know the ossification that was taking place just beneath his tongue. But why would he? In his small world, he was being a good husband by going down on his pathetic wife. He was always deaf and blind to who she was as a woman, a person. Now he was the taker of her soul.

Zaytoon strangled out the story's end.

'Iman, when he had had enough, he threw the plastic on the floor and rammed into me. Seconds later it was over. He was back at the table and on his phone. I stumbled to the bathroom.'

Zaytoon told me she never wore that lingerie again. It was boarded up with the pieces of her that died that night.

I sat there stunned, and so deeply hurt on her behalf. Part of me wanted to strike him with a rolling pin when he got home and part of me wanted to spit at his feet. I could do neither because I had to keep her secret.

At the end of all this, she managed to pull herself together and in a self-conscious fashion made the following startling confession, 'The next morning, Iman, I tied his lunch, sandwiches on top and samoosas wrapped in a very special, smoothed-out piece of clingwrap.' I almost imploded with restrained laughter; the agent of her humiliation was rescued from a dustbin in the kitchen and became a small but significant tool in her own revenge. Her wet smile told me she felt some satisfaction and justice and my smile bravely stepped out from behind damp eyelids.

I held onto her in a sisterly hug that tried to reach deep inside, to make contact with her precious, chilled heart and make it warm again.

We kept less and less in touch as I increasingly surrendered to Jozi and the chaos of my career. I learnt later that she was able to pull off the suffocating mask of unjust tolerance and obedience and finally breathed in the air of independence. She called to tell me that she did leave him and that once her family found out about his other life they supported her divorce. I still hurt when I think of her story.

19

When Sex is More Cursory than a Handshake

I lit a cinnamon-scented candle and turned the lights down. I had a feeling he'd arrived so I got up from my chair and walked a few steps from the darkened dining room towards the door, my feet padding softly on the carpet. I reached out to its round, silver handle, gently turned it and pulled the door open. My eyes fully expected to see a man strolling along the short walkway and up the stairs. That would have given me a few crucial seconds to compose myself and prepare my reaction to seeing him again.

I was to be denied those few seconds.

As our atmospheres interfaced, mine warm, his cold, he

was there. Standing in front of me with his hand moving out of his pocket as if to knock on the door. A look I could not quite decipher crossed his face. He seemed to have the appearance of someone trying to be invisible, trying to go unnoticed. Like someone who tried to walk through this life without leaving an imprint. Or maybe that's just the way he seemed to me.

We had only met once before.

The first meeting was drenched in alcohol and exhaustion but tonight I was just tired. It was late and I was leaving the US in the morning and heading back home to South Africa.

I looked for an energy that would identify him as alive, ambitious and invested in life but I couldn't find it. Perhaps it really was the timing. Our meetings weren't at the peak hour of fresh human interaction but in those suspended moments between midnight and morning.

As he stood there, the light from the porch added a warmth to him, its yellow hues lent him a false radiance. His striking blue eyes were the only remarkable feature distinguishing the space between his head, obscured by a low-set beanie and his body, insulated by a dark jacket.

The first time I met him it was his eyes that stood out. They seemed to single me out like they were boring into me, making the distance between us seem non-existent. They were magnetising. So when he offered me the spare tequila he'd originally bought for a friend who had disappeared by flinging himself into the gyrating mass of bodies on the dance floor, I'd accepted, even though I don't drink tequila and he was a stranger. In that moment I felt we'd said enough just by looking at each other.

A few frugal sentences later, 'Oh you're at Duke University? Where you from? South Africa? A journalist? Okay, wow.' 'Me? I'm from Wilmington. I work in a plumbing parts factory. We've just come out for some pool and a beer.' It wasn't long before we were splattered against a massive mirrored wall at Shooters, drink in my right hand, his face in my other. Shooters was a student hang-out and the music and the crowd were loud and sexy. It bulged and throbbed with young people, drunk, happy and borderless. Anything went. From volunteering to dance in a suspended cage to riding the ageing mechanical bull, no one cared about anything but having a good time. And in those moments neither did I.

The months previously had been hard and emotionally draining so I was ready for a reprieve of any kind. As I felt his mouth search for mine, I held his cropped brown hair and nudged his head in the right direction, trying to position him in a way that would benefit us both. The glittered disco ball sent slivers of light snowboarding off his face; it made him seem other-worldly. He hadn't said much and he didn't need to. I didn't want to know his background, his aspirations or why he was there. It was all about the flesh in that moment.

Looking back, I could probably count all the words he said to me and they would fit into my shoebox with plenty of room for a pair of shoes. He said, 'You're hot,' and that was enough.

But as we tangled into each other on that dance floor, I was stealing something from him. It was the thing I secretly wanted the most. It was what I always want. More than mutual lust or sex. I was after that special exchange of energy you can only ever experience when two humans touch with intention. I wanted to have sex, yes, but in my mind I also wanted a piece of him. A piece of him that would superimpose on a piece of me and be real, relevant and meaningful beyond the time that the sweat and semen of our encounter would be banished by the morning wash.

A few more drinks later and the lights came on.

It's the only time that a nightclub betrayingly transforms into a confessional. All your sins are laid bare as the effects of too much drinking are highlighted by the scene around you. Drunk girls and boys on the bathroom floor wasted, the sounds of spirited throwing up followed by soothing voices cooing, 'Watch your hair.'

Girls stood bare-faced, their make-up sweated off by over-zealous dancing or excessive making out. The liaisons decided upon in the secrecy of the dark and the loud music were exposed as people sheepishly exited with the person they planned to take home. The shine from their sequins less eager and less spectacular than just a few short hours ago when they left home.

I was exhausted, less so from expended energy but more from the realisation, yet again, that this, all this, was a mirage and in some ways desperate. I thought back to when I was nineteen, an age when things should have been about pure fun. But it wasn't me then; too young and too intense, asking too many questions that measured the world and found it wanting. Finding that the only consequence of diving too deeply into people and situations is like diving into a shallow pool and emerging with a crushed skull.

But standing in the middle of Shooters at this odd hour, we grabbed our coats and joined the rest of our friends standing under a faulty light in the parking lot. We watched through the buzzing flicker as giggling girls and boys stumbled towards their groups, trying futilely to look sober in front of a parked police car, while they plotted their next move.

And so did we.

We all knew it was time to go home. I knew I wanted no more from my tap maker from Wilmington. I knew that we had no more to share because whatever was possible was tested and expended on that grimy dance floor. But it was two a.m. and we were drunk so there was no real reasoning at this point. And so it was that at the first mention of home-made moonshine our touristic self-interest kicked in and we were all on our way to the home of Wilmington's friend, himself a plumber, whose granddaddy brewed the said bootleg that was apparently chilling in his downstairs freezer.

The plumber had extended the invitation so it would be rude to deny an honest invite, right? When would we ever taste real mountain-brewed moonshine, we asked ourselves. Who could deny a taste of something that fell on the wrong side of the law? It seemed too exotic to miss out on so there we were at around three a.m. on a Saturday morning, taking careful sips of the potent brew from a fat, clear jar in a stranger's kitchen, thousands of kilometres from Joburg.

Mixed with the fading night, the exhaustion and the alcohol were tangoing nicely and flicking everyone into comfortable corners. My friend Shay threw himself on a bed and sprawled out, his belly waving goodnight from under a tight T-shirt, while he snored lightly into a duvet cover emblazoned with the Coca-Cola emblem. Our German friend downstairs was sharing a cosy Lazy Boy with our host so it was just the two of us. Wilmington and I on a straight shot to any place desire deigned to take us.

We started in the kitchen. I was hoisted, no, flung, up onto the tumble dryer, with him making a frenzied but failed attempt to get at what was underneath the long, black dress with the plunging neckline I had chosen to wear that night. My old, maroon Doc Martens banged on the dryer as we resisted and succumbed to each other in an intensely oxymoronic way. Twisting and pushing and then pulling each other in till we realised the kitchen was a vulnerable spot and that the moonshine-parched revellers could come crashing through the door at any moment.

It made the search for an alternative spot even more essential so we made our way up the stairs and onto the couch alongside the bed Shay still lay sleeping on.

Wilmington's uninspiring kiss at the start of this crazy night should have been a major clue about the blandness of what would follow, but I, ever the optimist, hoped, no, believed it would get better.

I should rely more on evidence.

The collision of our bodies and expectation climaxed pointlessly to a sweaty entanglement of kissing and untidy groping. There was no sex because neither of us had a condom so there was an acceptance that things could go no further. I began the ritual of collecting lost earrings, shoes and self-respect and took sober steps out the front door and towards our car, with all my tired and bewildered friends accounted for and in tow.

Saying goodnight to each other was a sheepish, 'thank you very much, hope to see you in future', but we were both seemingly certain on the inside that this would be the last time Wilmington would meet Johannesburg.

Until now. My last night in Durham.

I had cooked and eaten my final meal in the flat I'd been calling home for the last few weeks. I assembled my excessive grocery shopping leftovers to give to friends and fed the last of my belongings, rolled sausage style, into an already bulging suitcase.

I was about to look around for the last time and head to the bedroom, when just before midnight my phone beeped. An email had arrived bearing an unfamiliar, difficult-to-remember address. It was the address of someone who wanted to remain mysterious. No gugu@gmail-type address but a series of numbers and letters I had never seen before.

'How's your trip going?' the message said. It was Wilmington.

Despite all evidence to the contrary, I react with a hint of excitement. Lost causes. I like them. I try to help 'find' them. It's a job I fool myself into thinking I am adept at. But good intentions at the ready I reply, 'All fine, leaving in the morning. You?' It turns out he's driving to Durham. Right now. In the middle of the night and so of course I invite him to come and say goodbye, despite knowing that I needed my sleep and him coming over would mean there would be none of that.

So here he is. Standing in front of me. His hand back in his pocket, waiting for me to give some kind of sign as to what was going to happen next. I was a mixture of sheepish and formal, parading the emotional contorting I had perfected over many years and experiences, like an expert in my field.

It was like we hadn't met before. We asked each other the normal top two conversation starters: 'How are you? What have you been up to?' Hmmm. 'Good to see you.' Hmmmm. Predictable. This was going nowhere. I take the lead, 'How about a hug? So good to see you again.' I'm lying. The last time we were together waves did not crash onto the shore, lightning did not scar the sky and choirs of angels looked away in embarrassment from the pointlessness of it all.

The hug is a fumble so I suggest the bed would be more comfortable. What happens next must be slowed down so that the seconds can be teased into minutes. The kiss, as it was the first time, is akin to the gnashing of teeth, with his tongue hiding in his palate and his lips stuck. I try take the lead, making an attempt at tenderness but all I get is a faster version of the above.

And so onto the grand finale and I say: 'You're prepared this time, right?' 'Right,' he answers, like someone determined to make up for a failed exam. I'm sure that if I had switched on the light I would have seen the colour of his shame. But on the rubber goes and so do we. There is no dance, no conversation, no lovemaking. No exchange of anything deeper.

After a few slight moans on his part, I realise it was over before it even began. I'm incredulous as I thought he was feeling self-conscious because he had kept up the movement, which now was soft and strange. I concealed my shock and gently moved him off me and he disposed of the remains in a basket next to the bed which meant I would have to confront it in the morning and relive this night one more time.

I lay there frozen. I have derived more meaning, sometimes even real pleasure, from a mere handshake. A handshake with its clear intentions, its warmth and conviction.

He leant back on the pillow. I leant back on mine. We lay silently; each disappearing into ourselves. Like ghosts that know they must go on searching for home. He turned over with the tattoos in tribute to his murdered father and brother on his left shoulder left for me to read. Rest in peace Johnny and Daniel.

Sleep crept over us like a spirit. I felt nothing. And then he was gone.

I have thought about Wilmington over the years; hoped the sadness I felt he had carried has been replaced with happiness. Despite its sepia-ness, I'm still thankful that he did leave a piece of him with me that night, a piece that, like a picture, I can pull out and look at every once in a while.

20

The Unicorn in a Field of Lame Racehorses and Other Stories

I once dated a guy, very briefly, who was so vain I swear he imagined women being slain in the name of the Holy Spirit when he walked past. Actually, he didn't walk, he glided and bounced lightly as if every road wore a red carpet and everything he did was being photographed or broadcast on live TV, sparking the mass mania of swooning women and rapturous applause. He was one of those men who attracted women like sun-parched female camels after a long desert trek, to a leafy, lush oasis. Poor gullible fillies who looked like they might bite each other just to be called 'his' woman or to show other women he was interested in them. This makes the fact that I too was beguiled even more vomit-worthy. You see, I consider myself quite pragmatic and rational in the field of attraction. I can suss out a guy quite well. I can tell if he is in need of a trophy or a partner, a mother or a sugar momma, a jumping castle or a library, a drive-through, a vacation or a permanent residence.

I can divine his intentions from the way he approaches me to the way he treats me on a date. But this time all my powers of discernment deserted me.

We met in a noisy, throbbing, smoke machine-assaulted club (first mistake). He was surveying the place like an architect might, as a site upon which a masterpiece is to be erected and he did it with the slightly bored oh-please-do-something-anything-to-excite-me kind of face that somehow caught my attention. I was attracted to his self-confidence and the fact (that I only found out later when I overhead him in conversation with his mate about the state of our country's politics) that he could string several coherent, intelligent-sounding sentences together. Mind you, the package he came in was also rather nice. He was tall, had a strong face and a yummy behind and a whiff of cerebral prowess. He asked me for my number in a charming, safe, non-line delivering way and spared me what we in Durban call the 'throw up'. That way of wooing a 'cherrie' with everything but your father's spanners.

Our first date was a chivalrous affair. Nice restaurant, my chair pulled out for me, dessert sharing and miracle of miracles, the bill was paid and not by me! I could feel the delirium rising. This was different to the cheap, tiring pattern that was starting to develop with other dates I'd been going on but that deserves a lot more time so I'll elaborate on that a bit later.

He drove me home (which was also a nice touch), gave me a tame kiss goodnight and his interest was piqued. Until I started to show interest back. The more attention I paid him, the less I got in return. Strange but in retrospect utterly predictable of the species who perhaps still need to act out the hunter-gatherer role, a role somewhat eclipsed by the onslaught of civilisation and the fact that women are not waiting on the front stoep of the cave waiting to be clubbed and carried off.

Later, his after-dark performance should have warned me further against him because even our nocturnal gymnastics were more about his stamina and agility than any meaningful, intimate exchange. The room might as well have been covered in mirrors and angled to show him only himself because he performed as if he were vying for a gold medal. The whole thing fizzled eventually because you cannot be with anyone who, when they stare into *your* eyes fool you into believing they are reaching into your soul, only to discover that actually, they are looking to see a reflection of *their* own image burnt on *your* retina. You cannot be with a man whose first and only love is himself. Narcissus had nothing on him, baby.

We once went to a nightclub together where, as usual, women were fawning all over him. Sisters, can you relate to this? Women who think they can hit on 'your' (I use the term loosely) man who is clearly with you, in your presence. The ones who dance overly enthusiastically, desperate to make eye contact, who give that fake-ass coy smile, acting all innocent and trying to accidentally/on purpose bump into him on the dance floor or try jiggling their tits and shaking their asses in his face, while you are watching.

No respect but so predictable. I find it amusing but at the same time irritating. Now, if 'your' man responds to that circus then you should have your head read for staying and tolerating that and pretending like you are blind. A man is not to be fought over, certainly not with another woman. Your beef should be with the idiot you are with not the sister that is trying her luck with him. She came with her hustle while you came with your man. How you leave is not up to her but up to you and the man by your side (if he's still there).

So this guy was loving all the attention because he acknowledged the play by smiling back or entertaining an 'accidental brush'. And I'm left feeling as stupid as a cat wearing socks watching it all unfold in front of me. What's worse is that we are in a neighbourhood, and at a club, where it seems he is one of only a handful of men with a fancy car, expensive apparel and cash. So he stands out. He might as well have had a bullseye on his back and a target on the front for those women who subscribe to attraction based on stuff and looks (a lot of us apparently). He clearly fancied himself as a unicorn in a stable of lame racehorses. Special, praiseworthy and utterly separate from the herd.

I dropped him soon after this and wrote the whole episode off to learning to not be so judgemental of women who date similar 'special' men.

This lesson was such a throwback to my youth and one I had clearly not learnt properly. When I was younger it was obviously the light-skinned, straight-haired, green or blue-eyed brown girls that won almost all the boys first while the rest of us were left to scavenge like hyenas around the slim pickings left after a kill. Or to focus our attentions more keenly on those who, while not exactly grabbing the headlines, had something special of their own. The politics of attraction were being learnt at church, at the club, on campus or on the streets and they would inflict wounds and scars on all of us. It's quite evident when you consider the kinds of childish games grown adults play with each other that prove even the most fundamental lessons of worth and boundaries are still being learnt.

It became fun after a while to create a 'lexiconman' for my girlfriends, for ease of reference about the types of men we would meet and whether we should catch and release.

The NGO: I suspect we have all encountered this particular type of man at some point in our lives. The earnest, well-meaning but completely out-of-pocket activist/student/in-between jobster/tight-budget tightrope walker who relies on his slogans and abundant charm to lubricate your interest and substitute the payment of bills.

I have had my fair share of these men and there really is nothing wrong with them ... to a point. Somewhere in my primordial state there was the expectation that at some point, at least once, 'the man' would step forward and offer to pay the bill or at least part of it. The trouble with some of these NGOs is that they spend your money as if it was theirs. I was once gobsmacked at the audacity of a guy I'd offered to take out to dinner because he had told me he was riding on rims. I thought it would be a nice gesture to take care of the bill so off we went. But brother-leader wasn't satisfied with a middle-of-the-road meal so it was the finest cut of steak and a parade of beers to match that made their way into his greedy mouth. He summoned the waiters with a flourish of his hands as if he were Louis the XVI himself with a dazzling crown atop his pompous head.

As the night wore on and his drunkenness grew, I found

myself thinking, 'What am I doing here?' But that's not all. I had been hoping the conversation would make up for the lack of couth on his part but even that was disappointing. I disagreed with him about something to the point where he raised an arrogant finger and shushed me. He actually shushed me and said, 'I am a Pedi man, Iman, I will speak first.' Well, that statement took me just seconds to digest before I summoned the waiter with a flourish of my own and brought the night to an unceremonious end. But not before further insult. 'Please could I have some money for petrol? I'll pay you back. I promise.' I'm still waiting for my two hundred rand.

I was done with brother-leader. So imagine my surprise when I got a call from him a week later, as if nothing had happened, asking if we could get together again. He didn't get far as I let the click of the phone provide the answer and I dragged myself back to the acceptance that I still had many more frogs to kiss before I found anything bearing the slightest likeness to a prince.

A prince possibly from any of the categories below.

The B and V (beige and vanilla combo): These men are what they say they are. Dependable. Reliable. But as bland as lite margarine. They move in a kind of predictable groove. They won't drop you from a dizzying height but sadly they won't make you touch the ceiling either, let alone the stars. They are where they say they will be, which is almost always at work or at their mother's house so you'll never have to panic and check their phones. But you have to decide if you want your relationship like you want your TV guide, with its suffocating predictability dressed in a checked dressing gown and stokies, as opposed to the almost death-inducing life-giving fever of a man who will make you go mental!

Of Dorbyl boots and Champion bags: My impression of these guys is that they are the sweat and muscle of honest, hard work, leaving early in the morning, arriving late, if at all, stuck out on a rig somewhere for weeks on end sometimes, applying their skill at boiler-making or welding. This guy formed the staple of labour from brown communities like Wentworth in KwaZulu-Natal. A guy as open as the quart he drank, with rough hands, a tender heart, clean vest and dirty mouth.

The *Glyer*: Hmmm. This is a special category. This guy is all big talk, little action and lives a champagne life on an Oros budget, as the boys in the hood say. He talks big, so big, yet arrives on a date via a bus or taxi, and every story he tells has to be split in half and further divided by ten. Why do these men feel the need to pretend they are something they are not when the truth is actually far more appealing? Brothers, you are trying, you are doing the best you can, just be yourself. Stop with the throw ups already. Mxm!

But the *glyer* doesn't stop there. He's probably going

home to a dark house with no power, which he shares with his mum and siblings, because while he may have found the money for Converse and Jack Purcell, bomber jackets and designer caps, he didn't find any for electricity. Damn fool.

The Lord's Yeah!: The perfect but oh-so-elusive man. The man who can make you swerve cerebrally and physically, who challenges you with his head and his heart. He has depth and height, he says what he means and does what he says. He won't make a sport out of making you feel stupid and uncertain. Um ... I've yet to meet him. Has he been created yet?

21

The Sexual Revolution: The Rise of the Commanderess-in-Chief

I am going to build one of those famous flyovers, definitely not like that engineering disaster of a highway in Cape Town that goes nowhere, but an elegantly efficient one that can neatly swoop over, let's call it the gaping, crocodile-infested chasm that defined my marriage, in the 'Imploding Years'.

When I met the Mr to whom I would become Mrs, I had largely carried the fear of God and plagues in respect of sexual dalliances. Of course there was the understandable dabbling in discovery and lightly dodging the licking tongues of hellfire so I was untouched (in the biblical sense) when I finally let my ex-husband cross the frontier. He was the only one. The anointed.

So when the complex of our union was torn down and demolished, leaving behind only smouldering heaps of recrimination and destruction, I found myself in the hinterland of fear and inexperience where these matters were concerned. When things fell apart, my sense of self and my confidence lay in the rubble amongst so many other things. I had to start with what was the most damaged, my self-esteem and my attractiveness as a woman. I had always been confident and sure of myself but I realised that actually I wasn't anymore.

But I'm not one to sit in a heap and ossify slowly. Especially if the invitations to the big pity party say 'ADMIT ONE ONLY'. Where's the fun in being miserable alone? My misery had to become something else and it soon morphed into militancy. C'mon girl! Take charge! You are the commanderess-in-chief of your own sexual revolution! You keep it all together for a man and then it's all for nothing. Hell no! Find that backbone, get out your gear, it's time to go to war! More importantly though, I had been coming round to the realisation anyway that the whole 'All-hail-to-the-hymen, marriage-is-a-covenant' bullshit was just another way to define a woman's self-worth by things that she did not always have supreme and singular control of. And it also seemed like a pretty backward value system. But there was a negative side to this Amandla state of being that was reactionary and not as thoughtful, as I would later discover.

I found myself out of practice in the gladiatorial amphitheatre of dating, where you have to dodge lion-like predators who are just hungry and thirsty and amoeba-like species that are looking to land and leech. So many types, so much to learn, I thought, as I began to dress for the battle. Two-storey heels (ouch), bustiers (gasp), clutch bags and slashes of red lipstick that I had to remember to wipe off my teeth. Egged on by my sister friends, I 'put myself out there'. The trouble is that hunting grounds are just that, hunting grounds, complete with dangers that require you to be prepared and to understand the game.

Was I the prey or the predator? I kept forgetting. I'd giggle to myself where the effort just seemed to be too much. Stand at the bar, at a strategic point and surreptitiously monitor the entrance. Act like you're not interested, that you're bored even and be obsessed with your phone. Sip your drink with your eye fixed on that screen. Lean in, let the girls peek over the rim of your top, let a little sexy bra show, flick your hair, lick your lips and look slightly cross. Or engage in serious conversation about war and hunger so that he knows you're a 'serious' person. Challenge him and then move on. Engage in this contradictory switching between interest and boredom and appear more out of reach than your brightly smiling, all-offering 'competitors' around you.

'Men like that,' the adapted *The Art of War* manual inside my head whispered. They like the chase. The harder it is, the more challenging they find it. It was an awfully taxing and tedious choreography for me. But it seemed to work and one night I got home, accompanied, and ready to follow through on, the purpose of all this preparation. But I hesitated. The guy was too slurpy, too eager, too, how shall I say it? Too stupid. But the game plan reminded me, You're not wanting to build a house and buy Royal Doulton tea sets with him, it's a shag! Get on with it and then throw him back into the pond!

Long story short. After an untidy mash-up of lips and tousled hair, buttons popping in the haste of undressing and collapsing onto the bed, I just couldn't do it. And perhaps I did the unthinkable by thinking too much about what should just have been a 'drive-by'. What would this single-use discard play give me, I thought? A sense of worth or shame? I wondered if there was anything beyond.

So much for the revolution. If I was leading an army they'd be left in the heat of the wilderness, starving and circling having sacrificed everything for the fervour of a single, now hollow-sounding 'Take the fight to them' slogan, willing to be martyred for a leader who was worse than insane but indecisive.

Then I thought, what's wrong if I was just myself? I

could be with whomever I wanted and it didn't have to be an act of war or defiance. It could just be about mutual need, an honest declaration that 'Hey, I don't want to have your babies but would you like to get sweaty with me?' That you didn't have to hate the person you were with, that you didn't have to punish him by proxy for the crimes of someone else but that you could actually be an adult about it. Say what you want, agree and get it.

And again what started out as rational, sensible and fair didn't come to a logical conclusion. It seems the men I met were not about honesty. They were seriously touched in the head. Baggage, lots of it, tied them down and tripped them up. If it wasn't an ex-wife and kids, it was about their 'notch in the belt buckle' rate and how many girls they could get by week's end. And don't even get me started on the married ones with their sob stories of 'my wife has just let herself go and doesn't appeal to me anymore'. Those I fantasised about taking home just so I could strangle them and do their wives a favour with the insurance money.

But then frustratingly I'd be hit with, in fact all my successful single girlfriends would be hit with this one, that classic, 'You're too intimidating.' A gem. Really? Reasonably speaking, what could intimidate a man about a woman who has her own point of view, is not looking for an ATM and is confident and not needy in any weird sense?

What's wrong with a woman who would like to be exempt from the games men play that are aimed at making sure 'that stekkie doesn't become too hectic' by not answering messages and then acting surprised and afraid when she asks for clarity and closure?

I've come to the conclusion (for now) that finding someone with sense, style, sass, good manners, and kindness with a sprinkling of 'street' is akin to going on an expedition for unicorns. Silence the horns, put away the bait and rather just stay at home.

But before I put on the expensive lingerie that I enjoy wearing just for the sensory personal pleasure and slide into bed with YouTube, a word to the brothers.

It's actually quite masculine and sexy to say how you feel. 'I like you, would you like to join me for dinner?' or to not be a douche when a sister asks you and just say, 'Yes, that sounds wonderful,' or 'No, but thank you so much.'

And, if and when, it doesn't work out as you'd planned, feel free to just say so in plain language. 'Thank you for your time but this is not for me.' Believe it or not, the women I know would not spontaneously combust or transform into Crazy Girl and eliminate you.

PUBLIC SERVICE ANNOUNCEMENT: PLEASE DON'T GO GHOST AFTER SEX. IT'S NOT NICE. Again, be skilful but honest. 'I'm not sure we got the alchemy just right but you were beautiful. Take care.'

The jury is out on whether I will ever be in a space with someone who wants the whole journey and not just the tourist attractions. And to all the sisters out there who genuinely feel lonely, you are not alone. I feel so incredibly lonely sometimes that my heart actually aches. Being cynical about men, if men are your thing, can be toxic. You will encounter all sorts but as my mum says, there's a lid for every pot, you just have to keep shopping.

For now I am actively making peace with the fact that it might just be me for me. It doesn't thrill me but it also allows me to move off the front porch, to relieve my eyes from the torture of staring at the horizon in case a figure appears and to just be fully present in whatever I choose to give my time to. I feel an empowering sense of peace and calm that this mindset has delivered to me. I'm by no means advising you to go quietly into that good night, or to snuff out your fire, but I also want to caution you that to fixate, to become impatient, may fool you into making a misguided judgement or desperation-fuelled decision that leaves you worse off than when you started.

I go out when the whim takes me. I create a memorable photograph of a moment here and there and I feed on it for as long as the winter of my isolation lasts.

Find a circle of good sisters who can talk you down from

the ledge of insanity. I have my three. We sit in our backyards, glasses of wine in hand and commiserate about our experiences. There are times when I've held court that I've expounded (cue academic voice) on my theory about 'The Fever'. When The Fever takes you, triggered by an intoxicating attraction to someone, you can't see anything beyond what you feel. You think, sleep, eat and speak in 'him'. 'He called me (giggle)', 'he sent me flowers (swoon)', 'he says he loves me (I'm dying as we speak)'. The magnetism is overwhelming. The whole wide universe, all of the galaxies and stars that you had before, are distilled into a minute fingernail of focus on the object of your affection. You're rendered deaf, mute and blind as to what is actually real about him and you exist in a manufactured, exaggerated fantasy.

You feed off his every text. You amplify his virtues; he seems more magical than he is in reality, and every kiss and touch has an otherworldly quality to it, until some time later, in the honest light of reason, you are able to see how ordinary and 'uncelestial' he actually is.

We laugh uproariously when I share this familiar sermon when one of the girls is trying to outrun a tsunami of feelings thoroughly distracted by a new beau. I encourage them to manage their fever, to keep it at bay, to not say or do anything triggered by it that they will regret or that will give that man leverage. The only anomaly in The Fever Theory is that when you are in the throes of it, everything feels more intense, more alive, more desirable and more addictive. As I conclude the sermon, I reassure them that no matter what we will be there, ready with the first aid kit to nurse them back to sanity, if it ends.

And finally, as we close the Council of the Grape dispensing advice with a perfect slice of cheese and fig jam, we laugh. And while I still can, I know everything is going to be all right.

22

And Now?

It is late afternoon and outside my window the sun sighs, preparing to lie down and rest after a busy day of marching in the same monotonous direction across the sky, dragging along a hot and heavy orb of light. As it kneels into a horizon greedy for its surrender, it leaves behind a cloak of dusk quite unlike any other I've seen in the world. My piece of Africa has a special, intense sky, made even more impressive by the silhouette of thorn trees, playful clouds and a family of hills standing still and watching in the distance. It seems appropriate that as I marvel at the scene, the powerful, pure sound of the Quran being recited crowds the room. It's a sound I once automatically associated with the majesty of creation and awe for God's artistry.

I stop for a moment to take in the chills that run up and down my body. It's been a long time since I remembered how it made me feel. The sound of Arabic recited in this way is able to take me by the hand, out of the house, past the front gates and all the way back to the first time I learnt how to recite it and how to wash and pray at a mosque in Queen Street. Those moments were magical. Even after all these years of surrendered faith, it makes my heart quiver.

I am coaxed into remembering the many hours I spent praying and supplicating. I smile as I recall my, shall we say exuberance, over the discovery of new faith. I was not content to do only what was necessary but what was desirable like fasting an extra Ramadan month to make up for the years I had lost in unbelief, as I thought then. Or staying up at night's edge to perform a special prayer called Tahajjud, which I was taught carried a special, mystical weight and influence with the Creator.

Religion was once my mainstay. And not just Islam. Christianity too. I navigated by it; when I lost my way, or lost myself and people, faith helped me find my true north once more. It guided a smile across the braille of sadness etched on my face. The music of Christianity helped me find the parapet above my suffering, helped me to peek over skyscrapers of problems; it taught me how to celebrate and give thanks. When I was feeling low (even now) I'd play Commissioned, The Winans, Larnelle Harris and Fred Hammond. Like the Qurannic recitation, it transported me to the special place where my knees once connected to the ground and my eyes were transfixed on heaven.

Faith and belief in God were my anchors; they were what made the ugliness and the meanness of life tolerable, they were what gave meaning and what inspired the hope for justice from those who had wronged you. It's an intoxicating space to be in, a place where your wrongs could be made right, where the sinful could forever expunge from their records their crimes and a place where the stains of vice could be washed away.

In this moment, the melodic recitation of a young Qãri is being applauded in a Majlis far away from my desk. Approving sounds accompanied by crying, encourage the Qãri. He is, in that moment, a reminder of God's instructions. Perhaps only a Muslim can understand just how deep, potent and provocative the Arabic recitation can be. It serves as an almost instant tug on the umbilical cord of faith. For those who don't know, it may serve as a way of understanding, even if you vehemently disagree, as to why millions are drawn to the faith and kept there by centuries' old teachings.

What I hear is one of my most favourite Surahs or

chapters, Surah Ar-Rahmãn. It tells the story of the generosity of God in making provision for his creation both on earth and in the afterlife. How ironic then that it is exactly these themes around which my enquiry was sparked; about man's origins and the question of whether someone/something omniscient and omnipotent made our existence happen in the first place and whether that being or beings is/are invested in every aspect of our lives.

But mainly it was the suffocation that I was beginning to feel in the most basic but important ways that fuelled my desire for the fresh air of a new place that would not make a disability out of being a woman. In my experience, the religion of Islam is set up to give men power over women. No matter how much I rationalised and reasoned and used the verses to justify and explain and make sense about a so-called 'complementary, mutualistic' system of coexistence and power sharing, I just did not find it or see it, and I spent many sincere years trying to understand. Believe me.

One afternoon, as was customary in the early days of my husband and me being in Iran, one of our teachers came over to 'talk of holy things'. I asked about the purpose of our invitation to Iran, which was to study Islamic jurisprudence and then to teach and perhaps lead. I wanted to know whether if I accomplished my goal of becoming a female judge could I make fatwas and would anyone be able to follow them? Further, could I become a religious leader if I had sound teaching and experience?

A sense of gravity covered his eyes; he gathered his heavy, brown robe across his chest and as he did so the burnished silver encasing his amber-embedded aqiq (prayer ring) caught the light. While it sparkled, I felt my own light begin to fade as he apologetically explained, 'Iman, no one can follow you. As a woman you can make judgements and you can follow them but no one else is permitted to do so.' It would be impossible then for me to even think about being a legal jurisprudent that led other women and men.

It would have been immodest to let my jaw hit the floor so I absorbed the impact of that explosive declaration by staring into the ground.

It can take many years to become a Mujtahida, but all those years of study and legal considerations could only benefit one person, me, just me, because I was a woman.

I thought about the brothers from all over the world who were attending the men's university with my husband. Why was I considered different from them? Our apartment was often the gathering place for furious religious debate and animated argument so I got used to insisting that I be a part of the discussions and not just be relegated to the kitchen to prepare tea and fruit platters or to listen from behind a curtain while the men had 'grown-up' discussions. I asserted my position early on because I thought I had to. I think it was a source of embarrassment and discomfort sometimes for some of the other wives who accepted that their silence was expected, or that their opinion be expressed in another forum. I think a lot of the time it made the brothers uncomfortable or feel pity for my husband for having such an 'ungovernable' wife.

The other prejudices around women further squeezed the breath out of me. For example, inheritance; giving men a larger share (I've heard many defences in this regard such as men have to go to war and must make provision for their spouses, women get a dowry; all problematic and outdated in modern societies, where it's women who bankroll the family or raise families by themselves), giving testimony (two women's versions of the same event equals one man's version) or marriage negotiations which seemed to suit men's terms (temporary marriages took place in many places I visited; you can be married for anything between one hour and 99 years without permanent obligation from the man and you could have more than one wife without permission or knowledge of the first).

But my disquiet began even before that. Early on in my marriage a petition was already being formulated for the inclusion of other wives. The scripture went from being my wellspring to being a weapon against my resistance. I reeled in shock. Why? Why are we here, ready to crowd our marital space that hardly has any miles on it, when we have barely begun to understand a complex faith? I spent many nights burying my face in a pillow, drowning it in tears after marathon, exhausting debates about historical context and the Prophet's conduct in the matter.

Later, I found myself in a polygamous marriage (the temporary sort) without my permission, with a woman who had pretended to be a dear friend. It's not a story that deserves any respect or further description save for the purpose of illustration. It was a situation that developed at my most vulnerable; when I was pregnant with my second child. It drove me mad knowing something was up but I had no proof, only to find out later and feel like a fool that all my fears and anxieties had been justified. It hit the truth home with a sledgehammer-like force that the Book, while beautiful in parts, could also become the 'How To' manual for sedimenting the position of men and turning women into chattel that must be left to compete for their affections. Most of the women I spoke to about this at some point or another, simply pulled their chadors tighter and whispered ever more softly, 'What can we do? This is our faith and we must obey.'

I have met too many Muslim women to mention who bear the pain of co-wives so deeply. It has scarred them, it has altered them forever, it has divided families and silenced them.

Religious patriarchy, to my mind, is of a special, distasteful type and it is especially exhausting because it gives divine sanction for men to wield power over women. It ascribes to them a patronisingly supervisory power over women, that through learning and experience goaded me towards pushing outside the (dis)comfort of faith. I had always promised myself that I would live my life sure of my intellectual and spiritual position, that the second it rang hollow, I would re-evaluate and then act. That the moment things ceased making sense or promoted injustice, that I would reconsider my position and move. This is precisely what happened. In the beginning, I was satisfied to see the practical laws as systems that enhance a harmonious society and I focused on the philosophical underpinnings of the faith. But as the laws began to have a material impact on how I was able to live, progress and aspire in society, as I began to live in a lesson, I realised that despite my best hopes, the truth was that I would never be an equal citizen in that construct and that it is the fragility of men it seeks to scaffold and muscularise. They are weak, so we must be weaker, we must speak more softly, look down and be more invisible as a mark of true womanhood. Their masculinity must be protected and catered to at all times, at all costs. And I could not do it any longer.

AND NOW?

I once conducted an experiment while I was living in the holy city of Qom to test my theory that the more women cover up, the more certain men will aspire to find out more. That no matter how you try to manage their reactions, it would not be enough. One day I decided to add a special head covering to my chador. It was the niqab, a covering that allowed only the eyes to be seen. Gloves on, wrists and feet covered, I was ready to hit the market. But contrary to my expectation that I would pass like a spectre through the throng, with each step I felt more observed. As I moved and looked up I believe I was more stared at than when I wore just the chador, the more conventional and common covering in the city.

I shook my head when I got home, convinced that when we make the obvious unreachable and untouchable, when we exoticise the normal, such societies become wired to make that which is off limits even more coveted and desirable, and fetishises the generally commonplace.

As I look back on these pages I've written and see with the benefit of looking from a higher place, or seeing from the outside, I know how much both faiths meant to me and how each, in its own way, fell short of reason and justice.

Mine was not a flirtation with the faith, neither Islam nor Christianity before it. I felt it. I believed it. I was at one point ready to die for it.

You couldn't live in Iran and not hear the horror stories

of the consequences of chemical warfare on their people. Grown men and women who are forever afflicted with severe nerve damage or those who still mourn the death of children in their mothers' arms, frozen in time as mustard gas in Saddam Hussein's insidious arsenal overwhelmed them before they had time to react.

Religion and martyrdom were once concepts that were easy for my mind to reach and my consciousness to embrace. I understood it. I would have sacrificed myself if asked.

One day after a particularly harrowing visit to a war museum I cried as I wrote the following song.

Muhammad Husayn

Little boy not yet a man
The earth for a bed, for a blanket a tank
In his hand a grenade his little heart unafraid
Muhammad Husayn we'll never forget your name

These are the fingerprints of our war
If this brother dies there are a hundred more
What is blood and what is pain
When we are the sons and daughters of Husayn

A mother stands behind her son, her only one,
Urging him on but what if he dies?

AND NOW?

With a smile on her lips and tears in her eyes ...

For these are the fingerprints of our war
If this brother dies there are a million more
What is blood and what is pain
When we are the sons and daughters of Husayn

O' my brother, surrender your soul
Life is half
Death is the whole
Don't be afraid of a little grenade
In the hands of the Creator you will live forever
Husayn Jannam
Husayn Jaan
Husayn Janaam
Husayn Jaan
Husayn
Husayn
Husain ...

Belief is a powerful thing. When it is coupled with righteous indignation and the desire to express it, it can be deadly.

It took a series of revolutions, convulsions small and big and spiritual and religious tectonic shifts to get me to a point where I slowly woke up to the irrationality and futility of a belief in a supreme being who was obsessed with whether we are ritually clean, how we have sex and with whom, what to eat or what not to eat, who is needy, clamouringly intrusive, jealous, invading our minds and thoughts, always needing our affirmation that HE is glorious and supreme.

It was easy to walk away once I'd got my mind right. I was exhausted anyway from keeping up the pretences of observing all the rituals. I had stopped praying about a year before I finally admitted I was done, but I was not ready to 'come out'. I was dealing with my own pain of separation, I was wrestling with the prospect of once more being out on my own without a spiritual tribe. So I washed and showed up on the mat but no prayer crossed my lips. I did not do it lightly and my time in Islam and Christ affected me deeply. They will always be two of my greatest teachers.

Today, I choose no label, no movement, no description. I know that, as someone said, you choose the strongest doctrine of the day and move with it until something stronger appears. That to me is the only supremely honest and rational way I think we can exist. But mine is not to preach. I leave that to the experts that preside over mimbars and pulpits but I do encourage a long hard look at the fruit of religion across the wasteland of injustice wrought by misogyny, racism, patriarchy, superiority and defence of doctrine, carried out in its name.

These days, the only religion I practise with any sincerity

is the religion of learning. My doctrine is shaped by what I see around me. It is all the proof I need that the world has to take an honest look at itself and decide whether we can live to serve each other or kill ourselves with division trying, ironically, to serve some all-knowing, patently needy celestial being. My attitude is that of using whatever means I have to question the enduring tyranny of political and economic systems that cast a gloating shadow over oceans of poverty, while preaching the virtue of that which only serves the powerful.

23

Which Face to Wear Again?

Most mornings I drive to work open. My mind and my heart are ready for a signal from the universe that I can build on and share with my listeners. A beautiful autumn leaf trying to hold onto the betraying surface of my windscreen loses the battle and whispers, 'Remember the seasons, things will always be in a state of change, Iman, remember me.'

As she joins the pile, wet and orphaned on the pavement, I race to my computer to encourage my listeners to hold on if theirs is a harvest of tears or to laugh as hard and as long as they can because a moment cannot be teased into forever.

On another day, I spot a homeless man, with his

dedication-etched face bent over near an indifferent street pole, brushing his teeth, taking such meticulous care it looks like worship. In a 60-second drive-by tutorial he reminds me that you can still have your dignity, your sense of pride in yourself, even if your heels are caked in dirt and your clothing is coloured in the brown-grey of poverty and rough living.

Once I stared at a man sitting on a pile of bricks near the wall of a cemetery along my route to work. He had fallen asleep and the most beatific expression rested on his relaxed cheeks. He was dressed for work and I mused about the journey that had brought him to that spot. It triggered a rush of images (all mine, I know) about where he lived, what time he'd woken up, got ready to be in this exact spot seemingly waiting for transport to get him to work. I wondered whose future rested in the hands clasped on his lap. Perhaps a child, a wife, a parent. It made me remember the toil of millions of workers in our country who show up and do their best inside a system that often seems to punish hard work or which anonymises the efforts of the ambitious who will never pierce the ceiling of racism or circumstance. I instinctively wanted to block the sun from his face, to shadow him a little longer so that he could dream a little more.

As I drive on I worry that, like running with a bowl of water in hand, I may drop or spill the exact reservoir of words I want to share to nourish the seeds of possibilities that lie expectantly in the gardens of my audience. I try to contain it, suppress it, keep it safe inside until I can set free a deluge of thoughts and emotions on a page for them to enjoy.

Sometimes the schoolroom of the road is not just for my audience but for me too.

One morning I had driven to work as usual after dropping my children at school. The night before had been tough. I had worked late and was kept up by my son, Muhammad, who seemed to be in great discomfort. I was worried. He was clutching his sides and complaining of pain. I wanted to take him to the hospital or call an ambulance but he waved the suggestion away. 'I can hold on until morning, I'll be okay, Mom,' he said. I wasn't convinced but I let myself fall asleep, while his sister watched over him. I was stunned to see the next morning that he'd slept in the Lazy Boy when I saw him under the blankets on the chair. His face was pale. He said he really needed to go to the doctor. I again offered to take him to the hospital but he assured me he'd wait until the doctors' rooms opened. I acquiesced, kissed him goodbye and left for the office. I phoned and made an appointment, I booked the Uber and in my head those dots were joined. I then dropped the girls at school, got to the office and began to write my introduction to the show when it hit me. You should be with your son! What the hell are you doing at work?

I withdrew my fingers from the keyboard. I pushed

out my chair. I told the station manager I had to leave. He immediately told me to go. I got into my car and drove to the medical centre like a person who believed that it was only there they'd find oxygen. Because I had stopped breathing. I was racked with guilt and worry. But this should be obvious, Iman! What's wrong with you? You are so good at joining dots, connecting spaces, how could you not see you should be with your boy?

And then it seemed that as I drove, a single word parachuted down and landed on the seat next to me. Just four letters. N-U-M-B.

I looked at it and I blinked. I looked at it and it swam away. Tears came hard and hot. I considered pulling over. I breathed in, I steeled myself and forbade the sheep-like following of any more tears. I tried to call my best friends but none of them answered. It was better that way. There were no distractions. Just me and numbness sitting together. Acknowledging each other. I heard from the back of my psyche, 'You are a shit mother'. It makes sense; those are the exact words I've thrown at myself. Those are the exact words my ex-husband has thrown at me.

My mind raced back to our December holiday. It came at the end of a series of long days holed up at Nasrec, where the governing ANC was placing a fresh mantle of leadership on a new head. The late nights and unending cycle of news had taken their jaded toll. My kids and I were ready to go to our happy place.

On the first day at the Durban coast, after we had enjoyed a satisfying taste of the ocean and had a conversation with the waves that went on for hours, the holes in our tummies dragged us out the water, into the car and straight to a curry institution in Durban. The Brittania Hotel. Thoughts of their bunny chows made our mouths flood with saliva.

As we drove there, there seemed to be a weird energy in the air. A bus overtook us in a reckless manner and my insistent hooting in protest seemed to directly offend the driver, who looked like he wanted to slow down enough to tell me off, or worse. As we dodged him we pulled into the parking lot. I wrapped my wet towel tightly around my waist, unbothered by the fact that I must have looked a sight with my curly, wet hair slowly defecting into a frizzy, blonde halo of an Afro. Sand stuck to my feet and legs like clingy toddlers and my children looked as if they had been swept to shore after a shipwreck; thoroughly dishevelled. As we strode towards the entrance of the hotel, an uncanny sight greeted our eyes. In a flash, I spotted a purplely-red sheet spread over something. It was a man's body and only his bare toes were visible peeping out of the bottom of the sheet. An ambulance was outside and a few waiters, who seemed to be in charge, were standing near his head. I took the scene in, stepped gingerly to the side and averted my little girl's eyes. We carried on, and into the arctic inside of the famous restaurant, listening to the gossip of other patrons who seemed to know the whole story. Slowly freezing under gale-force air conditioning I began to think and feel.

A woman leaned over and told me that she heard from the waiters that the man had been with of a group of friends and had spent the previous four days partying in a room upstairs. She added that she'd heard he had possibly overdosed and his companions had been panicked and brought him downstairs to get help but it was too late. I wondered what his friends must have been feeling and the sudden shriek of a woman, who seemed to be part of the group, confirmed the grief that must have been setting in. But like the other people in the restaurant we carried on, ordering our food and eating it.

By the time we left his body had been taken away. We got into the car and briefly discussed what we had seen, feeling sorry for this tragic turn of events so close to Christmas. But we carried on with our trip and soon the dramatic events were eclipsed when excited greetings were exchanged upon our arrival at my brother's home in Phoenix.

But the Britannia Man stayed with me. The scene kept returning and I worried how much my children comprehended what had happened. I had distracted them and diverted their attention and they hadn't really mentioned anything but I accused myself of indifference. Why did I think it was okay to carry on with lunch when someone had died? Why was I not affected?

After two wonderful weeks with family, we readied to return to Johannesburg. My cousins, Karen and Earl, were so excited to road-test their new car that they decided to join us on the trip back.

The ride was beautiful; South Africa is breathtakingly gorgeous. But not too far from the end of our journey I again saw a most incongruous out-of-place sight. It was a little girl's shoe lying in the middle of the highway. Time seemed to slow down. As I looked closer the reason became apparent. To the right there was a bakkie lying on its side. And in its chaotic veering across the highway, onto an embankment until it came to a standstill, was a trail of towels, bottles, pillows ... and bodies.

I pass the scene, telling the children to not look, and instinctively sprint to try go and help, with my cousins and aunt, who also stop, in tow. The sight that confronts us is grim and heartbreaking. A family, fresh from a seaside holiday it appeared, clipped a car that sent them careening off the road. Those I saw seemed to still be in their beach gear; a mother, a father and three children. The mother was pinned under the vehicle and the rest of the family had landed in positions that almost certainly spelt death or severe injury. Someone says they are trained in emergency response and they start to help. But the father is already gone, his one shoe separated from his foot with his leg impossibly contorted and bruised. He is covered with a blanket. A young boy moans and blood trickles down the side of his head. He's making a gurgling sound and is in severe pain.

And a metre or so away from him, is the reason I stopped. A beautiful little girl, with delicate blonde curls matted and defiled by sand, lying with her twisted, bruised feet in a pooling stream of petrol. I feel compelled to be with her but concerned that if I attempt to render any first aid I may do more damage than good. My mind screams for an ambulance so I call the office and send out a signal for help.

The poor thing lies face up, not speaking. She's in deep pain and shock. All I feel safe enough to do is stroke her hand. She is so little. There is no one else to watch over her and my mind races to my own young daughter. I would want to know someone would stop for her if we were ever caught up in the crash-chaos of a highway accident.

I am almost shocked by the tight grip she occasionally exerts on my hand. I tell her it's going to be okay, that she is not alone. My Aunty Alice finds her doll in the wreckage. It looks like it could've been a Christmas present and my aunt places it on her chest. It's small and pink. I try to sing to her. Someone says softly that the boy is gone. I choke, watching faces disappear from a family photograph and I am powerless to stop it.

I try not to cry as I sing 'Somewhere over the Rainbow' while tiny splinters of glass and small stones press insensitively into my knees and my bare feet are burning on the tar. I stroke her hand and tell her to stay with me. Over and over and over again.

Help arrives painfully late and we leave the survivors to try and pick up the pieces and find a new way to carry on on the journey of their lives. As we do ours.

As we drive away the death tally we have witnessed on our holiday totals three; two at the accident scene and one at the hotel. My mother has a superstition about threes; 'Everything happens in threes, my dear,' and I force my typically sceptical mind to agree because I so very desperately want the little girl, her mother and other brother to live.

The accident clung to me for a long time, like expensive perfume even after a shower. I wondered what happened to the girl and if her mother survived and how she was dealing with the heartache of grieving for her husband and son. But my heart was one degree separate. Forced to be so, after years of working with trauma. For my own sanity. Numb.

As I share them with you these three incidents seem to collide and I realise that this is what has been embedded in me. Not only through the trauma of what I have seen but also through what I have personally been through in my own life. There seems to be a layer of survival embedded between reality and my emotions. A dead zone where I live. A zone so thickly enrobed with scar tissue and inert nerves that I scarcely feel anything.

I experience joy and pain in a removed way, one layer short of really deeply.

As I drove to my son that morning, I wondered how long I had been half alive. I have developed this talent of pushing down, in organised layers, everything that hurts. Neat fold upon neat fold. Like clean sheets. I have developed a habit of expecting loss and misfortune, I have learnt how to not let it stain me. I know that I have a long way to go back inside to locate my 'original' self, like I suspect many others who employ abstraction as a tool to cope with and to handle pain. I'm open to the questions of how I landed here and am ready for the work of feeling, really feeling, again.

24

My Heart's Aperture is Wide Open

I'm so tired. It's been a long day. I feel sick. A migraine has decided it's time to torture me. My phone beeps. It's a message from Shams Alkhateeb. She's a mother just like me. And while our night-time fears around survival and the safety of our children are similar they are also starkly different. I fear a home invasion. I lock up and bolt the whole house, the electric fence is alive and the alarm is ready to cry for help if someone gets in. But thereafter I can usually wrap myself in luxurious linen, place my weary head on a pillow of down feathers and tentatively shut the world out for a few hours.

Shams, on the other hand, goes to bed unsure if tonight

is the night that fire and death will come, whether her family will be buried alive under rubble and destruction or killed instantly from the sheer force of an explosion gouging out chunks of their apartment building. Because, you see, where harmless clouds roll across the skies above my head, war planes, heaving with a deadly payload tear across the atmosphere above her home. She lives in Syria. In an area in Eastern Ghouta which has been under siege for more than four years.

We were connected through a series of simple, yet powerful, Twitter videos made by her two young daughters, Noor and Alaa. They are the sweetest and bravest girls. They take cautious walks whenever they can in their neighbourhood filming buildings that have been hit or talking to other kids whose only dream is to be able to go to school. They point the camera upwards trying to capture the sound of airplanes in the sky and the frightening noises of ongoing air strikes. Thousands of people have died and many children, just like Noor and Alaa, have been killed in a complicated, senseless war that pivots around power.

They tell the world they are afraid of bombing, that they are afraid of the planes. But the world does not have the ability, it seems, to change or influence their reality in a way that gives them peace. At least not for now. For now, all the rest of the world does is take grim records, writing down numbers and places. But once those numbers have names, faces, hobbies and dreams, once they are located inside a real story with an identity, we find it harder to be deaf and mute.

Here at home, I speak to mothers who carry their own figurative rocks on their backs or on their heads; a collection of burdens from traumas going all the way back to their own childhoods, of rapes and molestation, of beatings and deprivation. They wear the crimes of others on their bodies or deep within their psyches. We hoped that by now we'd have created a society in which children would never go to bed hungry. But they do. In large numbers. Inside a sewer-lined periphery of freedom.

Throughout my twenty years or more of journalism, I have found it hard to leave a story behind. As if it can end with a full stop at the end of a script. I carry the memories of families whose children are swallowed whole by a fire during the night, left to rock to and fro under a donated blanket wondering how they will live without their baby girl or boy whose body still has to be extricated once the flames are doused. I've seen bodies stretched out on a road on an early winter morning, lifeless, cold, alone, watching icicles form on their faces as the chill does its work. I have witnessed greed turn hearts into stone that become weapons of murder striking down a father and mother in their sleep. I've arrived at scenes where the blood of victims has not yet had a chance to coagulate, leaving me to speculate about the minutes before they died. If they knew they'd die, what would they have done?

There is a constant layering that happens to the observer, the collector of incidents, that cannot be undone or psychoanalysed away. As a journalist you can't unsee what you have seen. You can't sanitise the reality that you have proof of the depraved lengths humans will go to feed their lower selves. It stays with you. Each story. Each experience. Every time. And it alters you. It affects you. It's like taking out grim toys to play with that have been kept in a box of sadness.

Throughout my existence so far moments of ecstasy and horror and the unexpected fortunes and losses that come in the spaces between life's pendulum swings have made me practise speaking to others less harshly. Those moments have made me die a little more to the concept of my own ego with its desire to impose my ideas and thoughts with its proud swagger wrought by the superior belief that 'I know better' than others. I've not always succeeded and I berate myself constantly for regressing from the goal of living less judgementally. You cannot know how fragile life is if you have proof that that very day isn't guaranteed and live as if you have a thousand years, if you can gloat while your red carpet is rolled over the bodies of those you sacrificed for yourself.

I have laughed and I have lived, I have cried and I have sustained small, inner deaths along the way. I don't know what lies ahead. I have a sense of pride that through all I have done and experienced so far, I didn't end myself, even though there were times I desperately wanted to. I've even thought of the details. Where's good? A hotel? No, too strange; strangers rifling through my things, touching my body. No. At home? No, my children must not be burdened with a lifelong tragic image of me. Besides who would find me wherever I did decide to do it? There was no guarantee that it would be an adult who could protect them from the sight of my remains.

The enduring image that arrested me every time, that saved me every single time, was who would buy my youngest daughter a dress to wear to the funeral and who would hold her hand and walk with her to kiss my body for the last time? The idea still guts me so I am here, even when it is hard. Like it is for so many women and men the world over whose ability to fall asleep and wake up are like acts of defiance and victory over melancholy.

We grow up navigating by touch; blind in the darkness of an unknown future that tauntingly or delectably chooses to unfold moment by moment. You perhaps begin your life by framing a version of yourself that matches your idea of who you think you are. But that all changes though time and circumstance. I'm sanguine now about allowing my script to unfold, sentence by sentence, and I'm relieved that even though it's costly, my heart's aperture is wide open for the

MY HEART'S APERTURE IS WIDE OPEN

pain but also for the most indescribable beauty and pleasure that may enfold me in its arms ...

Acknowledgements

Our families are often our first teachers on the subjects of love, decency, conflict resolution, kindness and loyalty. And I have had some of the finest teachers. Starting with those whose lives are now pictures in an album, but who continue to speak through memory.

Daddy, I miss you EVERY SINGLE DAY. You are still my original hero. I feel your love. Of all the doctrines that make no sense, I will hold on to the childlike belief that you can feel my love too, wherever your spirit may be in the universe.

Aunty Eileen, you broke my heart when you died. I feel

cheated that I never got to have a last gut-tearing laugh with you ... don't worry, Maureen, Alice and Karen still carry your legacy, 'donkeytitis' (that inability to keep anything in, as secrets were blurted out and surprise birthday parties revealed because 'the donkey kicked your chest'). I love you.

Leslie, my beautiful brother, my eyes were opened to who you really were so late, I never really got to know you deeply. And I feel cheated for that. I carry your smile and spirit deep inside.

Anthony, you didn't think you were a teacher but you schooled me on so much. I learnt from your friends how much you loved me. Your last months were painful and traumatic and you disappeared inside yourself. But now your spirit is free.

Uncle Reggie, I will never, ever forget your generosity. As I wrote in your eulogy 'charity wears soft slippers' ... you cared for us and loved us so quietly – but your generosity shouted so loudly. I love you now and forever!

And now, to the physically living.

Mummy, there's a whole chapter for you, I know, but I want to remind you that it is YOU who made us so awesome! I learnt how to cook, to have respect and to never stop trying from you.

Eugene Rappetti, I look forward to your calls every day, which with their quick hello, how are you are as potent as

ACKNOWLEDGEMENTS

an hour of forensically detailed exchanges. I love how we can drink masala tea together and talk like adults and then transition into jesters, joking and laughing and being kids together again. Thank you so much for always protecting me, always caring for me. You are not a man of many words, but your consistent kindness can fill libraries. I love you so much. I am proud of you.

Jenny, my beloved sister, your gifts are so many. Thank you for sharing them with me over the years. You are more beautiful than you believe you are. Let the world see more of your wit, your talents and I hope that one day you get to say, 'I did it ALL!' I love you.

Karen Plaatjes, my sister from another mother. All those nights of nursing your asthma and squashing up in a bed with your mother are times I hold so dear. We have laughed and cried together, we have shared dreams and secrets in a beautiful dance of the bond that is closer than that shared by sisters. Thank you for loving me and I love you always.

Aunty Alice aka 'The Golden Heart' Endley. You, my special aunty are the one I ran to as a teenager, confessing things I wouldn't dare say to the other matriarchs in the family. You are still that person for me, the one I know will hold me close, affirm my strengths and set me on the road again, whole and in charge. Thank you for stunning goodbye breakfasts and for being so beautiful. I love you.

Malika Ndlovu, another sister from another mother. You made me believe hard in the possibility of freedom and self-expression. You helped me believe my own voice when I thought I was going mad! Thank you for sanity and loyalty. I love you.

And on to my sister circle.

Khadija. From the day we met gladiatorially wearing chadors, sparring over religion, with me being an impossible extremist, you bore my 'heaviness' and crept into my heart. That is where you have lived all these years. I value your wit, your humour and your loyalty more than any treasure. Thank you for teaching me not to shun my sultry self and to believe in true love.

To Sumitra and Marion, now exactly where would I be without a ready glass of wine, fresh crispy vedas, and arms always to stroke my head and share advice? It is thanks to the pair of you that I maintain my daily sanity and remember that tomorrow always comes, and with it new adventures and new reasons to be alive. I love you both.

To my original sister circle: Meena, Fathima and Ishara. You girls were on that tumultuous path with me navigating first love let downs, dramatic Bollywood-like suitors, family squabbles, heartbreak and loss in the streets of Unit 13. Meena, thank you for teaching me how to cook my first fish curry, and thank you for always creating a soft space for me

ACKNOWLEDGEMENTS

to land. You taught me starkly what true friendship means. To all you wonderful ladies, thank GD our friendship has stood the test of time!

To the Lenarea High School class of 1989 (damn, now I'm giving away my age), it was wonderful reconnecting with you recently. You boys played brother and protector to us and gave us a sense of family. I'm so grateful for the impact you had on my life and for still being genuine and faithful friends.

To the Youth Committee of Living Waters Church, Craig especially, you helped me believe in myself as a teenager and you gave us all such a wonderful platform for growth. Your heart has always been in the right place.

To dear friends such as Marilyn, Tessa, Robyn, Odette, thanks for looking over some of my words to ensure 'Quality Control'. To my other heart holders: Deanie, we spent many months not knowing if we'd make it out of grief alive but WE DID! Thank you to Poppy for being available for school pick-ups at a moment's notice and for feeding my kids when I've needed to travel. Sherwin and Verene, my day one people! Thank you for being ready with an ear and a shoulder. I treasure you. Dr Thandi Ndlovu, thank you for creeping into our lives and our hearts. My family owes you a debt of gratitude. I love you.

To the million friends who I haven't mentioned here, I'm pinching myself that I know you and that if I call, you'll be by my side in a hurry.

To new friends Given Mkhari and Andile Khumalo, you are more like brothers to me. Thank you for treating me like family and for allowing me to talk to the beautiful listeners of POWER 98.7.

And to the listeners, readers and viewers who I have had the privilege of interacting with over the years, thank you for giving me permission to do my work without fear or favour. Without your support my career would not be what it is. I bless you for giving me the opportunity.

And where would I be without the magnificent team of warrior women at Pan Macmillan? Thank you to Terry, Andrea, Jane, Katlego, Nkateko and the rest of the team, who have held me and my story with such care and respect. You have treated me with kindness and consideration, and I hope many more debut authors are able to work with a sisterhood like yourselves. Much love …

And to the man in my future, get here already. My heart is ready.